Becoming a Confident Quilter

LESSONS AND TECHNIQUES PLUS 14 QUILT PATTERNS

Elizabeth Dackson

Martingale®
Create with Confidence

DEDICATION

To my parents: I would never have even dreamt of writing a book if you hadn't instilled in me the idea that I could do whatever I put my mind to. Thank you!

To my husband: I couldn't have done this without you. Your belief in me kept me going, and having your support meant the world to me. I love you so much.

Becoming a Confident Quilter:
Lessons and Techniques Plus 14 Quilt Patterns
© 2013 by Elizabeth Dackson

Martingale®
19021 120th Ave. NE, Ste. 102
Bothell, WA 98011-9511 USA
ShopMartingale.com

Printed in China

18 17 16 15 14 13   8 7 6 5 4 3 2 1

**Library of Congress Cataloging-in-Publication Data
is available upon request.**

ISBN: 978-1-60468-231-1

Mission Statement

Dedicated to providing quality products and service to inspire creativity.

Credits

PRESIDENT AND CEO: Tom Wierzbicki
EDITOR IN CHIEF: Mary V. Green
DESIGN DIRECTOR: Paula Schlosser
MANAGING EDITOR: Karen Costello Soltys
ACQUISITIONS EDITOR: Karen M. Burns
TECHNICAL EDITOR: Ellen Pahl
COPY EDITOR: Melissa Bryan
PRODUCTION MANAGER: Regina Girard
COVER AND INTERIOR DESIGNER: Connor Chin
PHOTOGRAPHER: Brent Kane
ILLUSTRATOR: Lisa Lauch

CONTENTS

Introduction   4

Modern Quilting 101   5

Fabric   6

Tools of the Trade   9

Rotary Cutting   14

Exercise 1: Cutting with Confidence   14

Piecing Basics   16

Exercise 2: Finding the Sweet Spot for Your Scant ¼" Seam   17

Pressing   18

Exercise 3: Pressing 101   18

14 Patterns to Build Your Quilting Skills   19

Patchwork Dreams   21

Precious Stones   25

Sophisticated Square   27

Less Is More   31

Monterey Square   35

Refreshingly Retro   41

Polaris   45

Diamonds Are a Girl's Best Friend   49

X Marks the Spot   53

Rainbow Cakes   57

Lattice of Stars   61

Deconstructed Beads   65

Wonky Fences   69

Wham   73

Finishing Your Quilts   81

The Backstory: Backings and Labels   82

Preparing for Quilting   83

Machine Quilting   85

Binding   88

Caring for Your Quilt   90

Reading Quilt Patterns   91

Resources for Modern Quilters   93

About the Author   96

INTRODUCTION

So you're interested in quilting . . . this is absolutely the perfect book for you! You'll find all the essential information and guidance you'll need, from collecting the necessary tools to getting your feet wet with introductory exercises, and then making your first quilt. Even if you've made a few quilts already, this book is full of tips and tricks for every step of the quiltmaking process, to help build your quilty confidence.

Quilting has a long history, the details of which are beyond the scope of this book. Early quilts were not constructed as art or even as heirlooms; they were constructed for the purpose of keeping people warm. After World War II, quilting was viewed as old-fashioned and dated. To some, it was associated with the Great Depression and tough times, when one had to "make do." In the 1970s and '80s, however, quilting and many other crafts began making a comeback. Many women, the granddaughters of quiltmakers, developed an interest in learning to quilt. Techniques for making quilts were updated and modernized.

In this book there are 14 modern quilt projects, beginning with the easiest and progressing in skill level with each pattern. The quilts showcase some of the wonderful modern fabrics available at quilt shops and online. It is my hope that this book will serve not only as a reference volume that you can turn to during your life as a quilter, but also as a workbook that you can progress through, honing your skills as a quilter and stretching your creativity as you go.

Many people have learned to quilt as a leisurely activity that gives them joy. Others may have family members who quilted and want to continue a tradition. Still others find quiltmaking to be an artistic endeavor. Whatever reasons lead a person to quilting, it is a truly rewarding hobby, boatloads of fun, and something that anyone can do.

Happy Quilting!
Elizabeth

MODERN QUILTING 101

FABRIC

Fabric is the best part of quilting for almost any quilter; most of us are fabric-a-holics. My aunt used to have a bumper sticker on her car that said, "The one with the most fabric wins!" Many quilters build up a stash of fabric they love—yards, half yards, fat quarters, and more—and then they "shop" from their stash when working on projects. This isn't necessary to becoming a quilter, but it can definitely be a fabulous side effect!

A healthy stash of fabric includes all the colors of the rainbow.

When shopping for fabric, keep the fiber content in mind. Quilt-shop quality, 100% cotton fabrics tend to work best, although many modern quilters incorporate linen, voile, and flannel fabrics into their work. Knit fabrics don't work well in quilts because of their stretchiness. When you're starting out, I strongly suggest working strictly with cotton.

Why cotton? It's the most forgiving fabric to work with when you're learning. Not only does it tend to be quite durable, but it usually holds color well, which is important when you're planning to use a quilt for a long time to come. Once you feel like you've gotten the hang of quilting, then by all means, throw some linen into your fabric choices, or back a quilt with flannel.

As with many items, you get what you pay for with fabric. The fabric you find at a big-box or bargain store is often made from greige goods (the name for the base cloth) with a loose, rough weave that feels scratchy or appears thin. These fabrics tend to shred and fall apart easily, and the colors often bleed or fade. Cottons purchased from quilt shops consist of higher-quality greige goods, giving the fabric a softer "hand," or feel.

You'll also find that quilt-shop cottons tend to be more colorfast than their bargain counterparts. At the end of the "Resources for Modern Quilters" section on page 95, you'll find a list of fabric manufacturers and online fabric stores offering high-quality quilting cottons that will produce great results. And, of course, there's nothing quite like exploring the gorgeous goods at brick-and-mortar quilt shops in your area.

Fabric shopping can be a challenging process simply because there are so many choices! Among solids, for example, you'll see every color you can imagine, from rich jewel tones to calm, cool neutrals. You might not automatically think of solids as being visually interesting, but they are major players in the bold, graphic designs of modern quilts. Then there's also an amazing array of prints available. When you're browsing for fabric, you'll find that printed fabrics tend to fall in one of four different categories.

Tone-on-tone prints. Tonal prints tend to "read" strictly as one color and may appear solid when viewed from a distance, depending on the amount of contrast between the color values. For instance, each fabric in the photo below reads as just one color because there are no other colors in the print. One fabric contains only various shades of blue, another has shades of red, and so on. These are great fabrics to use in any quilt and definitely ideal candidates for building your stash.

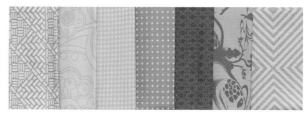

Modern tone-on-tone prints

Tone-and-white prints. This category is also full of great staples for your fabric stash. Tone-and-white prints can include many stripes, polka dots, and other fun repeating designs. One thing to pay attention to with these prints, however, is the shade of white—sometimes it's a very white-white, or bleached white, while sometimes it's more of an off-white. This is only an issue if you are particular about having a specific shade of white within your chosen quilt design.

Tone-and-white prints

Small-scale prints. Small-scale prints tend to have one primary background color with an occasional addition of another tonal color, white, or even different colors altogether. The background color is typically the most dominant color in the print.

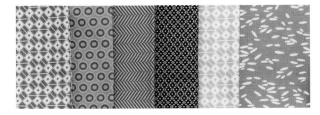

Small-scale contemporary prints

Large-scale prints. It's easy to be drawn in by the beauty of large-scale prints, but they often have strong background colors and/or supporting accent colors that make them a bit difficult to use. Large-scale prints are great to grab and plan your quilt around, however!

Large-scale modern prints

As you're fabric shopping, either in quilt shops or online, you may fall in love with certain fabric designers and manufacturers. I suggest that you look them up online and bookmark the websites of your favorite fabric manufacturers. Most of these websites include lots of eye candy from past and upcoming fabric collections, as well as information about where to purchase the fabrics. The companies may even share many free quilt patterns to inspire you.

CHOOSING FABRICS FOR A QUILT

There are lots of different ways to put fabrics together for a quilt. I often have a color scheme in mind, or I'll start with a large-scale print that I've fallen in love with. From there, I purchase additional fabrics or pull fabrics from my stash based on the chosen color palette or the palette from that large-scale print. If you look at the selvage (the narrow, tightly woven edge that runs along the length of the fabric), you'll see small samples of each color used in that print. Those color breakdowns can be helpful in choosing additional fabrics. Here are some of my other favorite methods of choosing fabrics for a quilt.

Fabric collections. A fabric collection is a group of fabrics created by one designer. The idea is that all elements of the collection work together harmoniously, with complementary colors and designs. You'll usually find varying color palettes with some type of cohesion across the collection, such as an overall theme. Most have some staple designs, like a stripe or polka dot, as well as larger-scale designs, such as a floral or tone-on-tone botanical print. Collections can have anywhere from 8 to 30 different designs, or even more, so working within just one fabric collection is a great, easy way to get started.

What's a Precut?

Precuts are exactly what they sound like—precut squares or strips of coordinating fabrics, in specific sizes, usually from a single fabric collection. Many fabric manufacturers produce these for fabric shops, and many fabric shops also create their own precuts.

Mixing and matching. You certainly don't have to use fabrics from just one collection. Mixing and matching fabrics from various designers and collections is a fantastic way to make a one-of-a-kind quilt. I find that quilts incorporating a variety of fabrics often have more depth and visual interest than those made exclusively from one fabric collection.

TO PREWASH OR NOT?

Many new quilters ask the same question: When you bring fabric home from the quilt shop or you open a wonderful box of fabric from your favorite online retailer, should you wash it or not? The answer is, that depends! Many quilters prewash all of their fabrics before using them, citing the fact that some fabrics do bleed and that various fabrics shrink differently. Others prewash to remove sizing and other chemicals that quilting cottons are treated with.

I am not a prewasher for many reasons, one of which is that I'm lazy! It takes time to wash and then iron your freshly laundered fabric. I've also never had a fabric bleed and cause problems, but to combat that possible issue I always toss a Shout Color Catcher in the wash with my quilts. These sheets, available in grocery stores, absorb excess dyes in the wash water to prevent migration of color into other fabrics. Alternatively, you can use Synthrapol, a liquid that when added to the wash water acts to prevent other fabrics from absorbing excess dye. You'll find this product at quilt shops and online.

Another big reason that I don't prewash is because I really love the soft, puckered look you get from laundering a finished quilt made of never-before-washed fabrics.

Stash Building

Having a stash of fabric is one of the perks of being a quilter. I often find a lot of inspiration from the beautiful fabrics in my stash. Beginning quilters tend to buy fabric specifically for a certain quilt project, but as you stitch up more and more quilts, you may find yourself accumulating fabrics simply for the sake of having them, even if you don't know what you're going to use them for. Or, you may purchase fabrics for a dream project that you intend to undertake far ahead in the future. Either way, here are a few key points to keep in mind when stash building.

- **Quality is important.** Fabric is an investment, so stick with quilt-shop-quality fabrics from respected manufacturers.

- **Buy a variety of prints.** When I first started stash building, I realized I was almost exclusively buying polka-dot fabrics, so unless you're planning an all-polka-dot quilt someday, go for variety. Pick up some large-scale prints, some stripes, and some tonal prints.

- **Buy a variety of colors, as well.** Just because you don't like orange today doesn't mean you won't need some orange in the future. My tastes have changed quite a bit since I first started saving up fabric. Just respect the rainbow in your stash building and be sure to represent all of the colors.

- **Half-yard cuts are the most versatile size** to have in your stash. They are usually wide enough and large enough to bind a lap quilt, plus they are big enough to use in making many quilt blocks.

- **Purchase what you love.** Don't pick up that bargain print just because it's a steal—pick it up because it's a color you need in your stash or it's a print you feel passionate about.

If you've been to a craft or quilt store and visited the notions section, you know that there are hundreds of notions and tools available for sewists and quilters. In this section, I'll run through the basic tools that you will need to get started in quilting, as well as some handy extras that are nice to have, although completely optional.

An assortment of essential quiltmaking tools

SEWING MACHINE

Any sewing machine can be used to piece quilts. You don't need a fancy, high-end quilting machine. Just be sure to keep your machine in good working order and have it serviced regularly. If you don't already have a machine, visit a local sewing-machine dealer and perform a "test drive" before making a purchase. For the record, I used a Husqvarna Viking Sapphire 835 to make the quilts in this book.

THESE FEET WERE MADE FOR QUILTING!

There are three different specialty presser feet that you may want to invest in as a quilter: a ¼" foot, a walking foot, and a darning foot. Please allow me to introduce them.

The ¼" quilting foot. This foot, also called a patchwork foot, is designed to help you produce a consistent ¼" seam allowance. The right side of the foot usually has a metal or plastic guide to align the raw edges of your fabric against. You may need to experiment with your foot to ensure that you are sewing a scant ¼" seam. (You'll find more about this, along with an exercise to help you sew a scant ¼" seam allowance, in "Piecing Basics" beginning on page 16.)

The walking foot. A walking foot, also known as a dual-feed foot or an even-feed foot, helps fabric layers feed evenly through the machine. It does this by gripping both the top and bottom fabrics during sewing. A walking foot can prevent slippage as well as puckers when applying bindings and machine quilting. I use this foot for straight-line machine quilting and attaching binding as well as other sewing applications, like stitching a handbag. It's also helpful when sewing slippery fabrics, such as voile. Many quilters use a walking foot for regular piecing. Some sewing machines even have a built-in walking foot.

The darning foot. This foot, also called a spring-loaded free-motion quilting foot, typically has a clear plastic or metal "toe," or window, allowing you to view your stitching. This is ideal for free-motion quilting, as is the spring mechanism that helps keep your fabric flat and under control. See page 85 for examples of free-motion quilting.

A ¼" foot, darning foot, and walking foot (left to right). Depending on the make and model of your sewing machine, your presser feet may look slightly different from those shown.

THREAD

For piecing, always use 100% cotton thread. Why? Cotton is the easiest thread to work with when quilting. It also has the same fiber content as quilting fabrics, making them a good match for durability. Cotton thread has very little stretch to it and gives a soft look when used for quilting, which is perfect for a quilt that's made to be loved.

Keep in mind that when it comes to thread, as with fabric, you get what you pay for. Inexpensive thread has a tendency to break easily and will leave behind more lint and remnants in your machine than high-quality thread. You may need to try a few brands to find the right thread for your sewing machine. Mine, for instance, loves Aurifil and Gutermann threads.

Try to use a neutral-colored thread for piecing; I tend to use white for all my piecing, with a few rare exceptions.

For machine quilting, you can use the same 100% cotton thread that you use for piecing, or purchase thread specifically designed for machine quilting. I like to use Aurifil 50-weight thread because it is mercerized to reduce fuzz and lint buildup in your sewing machine.

For hand quilting, be sure to choose a cotton thread designated for that purpose, as it will be glazed or coated for ease of sewing through multiple layers. *Don't use hand-quilting thread in your sewing machine*, because the coating on the thread will damage your machine.

NEEDLES

For machine piecing, use a sharp Microtex needle or a universal needle. A sharp needle has a thinner shaft than a universal needle, but either is fine for machine piecing woven quilting cottons. You'll want nice, straight stitches, so use whichever one works best in your machine.

For machine quilting, you can use sharp needles or quilting needles, which have a specially tapered point that allows you to stitch through multiple layers of fabric with ease. They are designed to work with high-quality quilting

cottons and prevent fabric damage. Needles do indeed dull with use, so be sure to change your needle after every 6 to 10 hours of sewing.

In addition to machine needles, you'll need hand-sewing needles. To finish binding by hand, I like to use Sharps or milliner's needles, which are longer than Sharps. Both have round eyes, which are easy to thread and will glide through fabric smoothly.

ROTARY CUTTER

A rotary cutter is a more dignified and worldly cousin of the pizza cutter. It's like a rolling razor blade, so always exercise caution when using one. A rotary cutter is used in combination with specially designed rulers to make quick, accurate cuts across the width of fabric. Rotary cutters are available in several sizes; a 45 mm blade is the best for all-around use, though larger and smaller blades are available. Select a rotary cutter that feels comfortable in your hand, and purchase replacement blades from the same manufacturer to ensure compatibility. Many rotary cutters offer various safety features, such as a safety lock to close and cover the blade when not in use.

You'll know when it's time to replace your blade—when your rotary cutter begins to cut poorly and you find yourself using extra elbow grease to cut your fabric. I try to replace my blade after every two quilts.

CUTTING MAT

To cut with a rotary cutter, you'll need a self-healing cutting mat made of thick, durable plastic. Most mats are printed with a grid on one side. They also have a bit of a rough surface to help grip the fabric and keep it from moving while you're cutting. Select a mat that will fit your work area, but keep in mind that the most versatile mat size is 24" x 36". This will accommodate any cut of fabric if you fold the fabric from selvage to selvage. Cutting mats warp easily, so keep your mat flat at all times, away from direct sunlight and other heat sources.

RULERS

For measuring and cutting, you will need clear acrylic rulers designed for use with rotary cutters. These rulers are marked with thin lines for measuring your fabric as you cut. The 6" x 24" ruler is an all-purpose size that will serve you well. The 24" length lets you measure across the width of fabric once it is unfurled from the bolt, and it's useful for cutting long strips of fabric. Square rulers, such as a 12½" x 12½" size, are super handy for squaring up your quilt blocks. I like Omnigrip quilting rulers, which have neon lines that are easy to see on a variety of different shades of fabric, and a nonslip surface that helps me keep my cutting as accurate as possible.

IRON AND IRONING BOARD

How well do you know your iron? It's pretty safe to say that any iron will work for quilting—but beware the old, dirty iron and the angry, spitting iron. If you usually press shirts and clothing with steam, your iron may be harboring some gunk on the soleplate. Be sure to use a clean iron on your beautiful quilt fabrics! A standard ironing board will do fine; it's actually just right for ironing large pieces of fabric. A travel-sized ironing board can also work well when piecing and pressing blocks.

BATTING

Also known in some parts of the world as wadding, batting is the material in the center of your quilt sandwich, between the quilt top and the backing. Batting provides warmth to the finished quilt and also gives dimension to your quilting stitches.

There are nearly as many different brands and kinds of quilt batting as there are fabric manufacturers. The three primary types are cotton, cotton blend, and synthetic. All of these come in various lofts; loft refers to the thickness or thinness of a batting, ranging from low loft to high loft. Batting made of 100% cotton is very easy to work with, breathes nicely, and gets softer

with every wash. Read the package carefully to determine how far apart your quilting stitches can be. Cotton-blend batting is also quite popular and is available in various lofts.

Generally, for machine quilting, stick with a low-loft batting, but for hand tying or hand quilting you can experiment with a higher-loft batting to create a puffy look. I don't recommend the use of synthetic batting, as it is often prone to bearding—the long fibers work their way through the fabric of your quilt and may create a fuzzy appearance on your quilt top and backing.

Remember how I don't wash my fabric before I use it? I don't prewash my batting either. That way, when I wash a finished quilt, the batting and the fabric shrink simultaneously and create a crinkly, puckered, vintage look. This is another reason why I like cotton batting—it shrinks at approximately the same rate as the quilting cottons I use for my quilt tops and backs.

PINS

As a quilter, you'll definitely use your fair share of pins. I keep two kinds of pins on hand at all times: regular straight pins and longer straight pins with flat heads. Straight pins are easy to find at your local craft store and come in a variety of widths and diameters. I tend to use 0.5 mm pins, because they glide through my fabric more easily than thicker pins. These are often called "silk pins." The longer pins have a flat head, often something cute such as a flower or butterfly, which make the pins easy to grab.

A Word about Pinning

Although I do keep pins on hand at all times, I often don't bother using them when piecing. With small pieces of patchwork, I find that I can hold the raw edges together just fine without them. I do tend to use pins for long pieces, such as sashing and borders, and when I piece curves. Experiment to find what works best for you.

MARKING TOOLS

You will need some fabric markers or pencils in your quilting arsenal. Marking utensils are used to draw lines on the wrong side of squares for making half-square-triangle and flying-geese units. Several kinds of marking tools are available, some with water-soluble ink and others with disappearing ink. Frixion pens are another option, a standard office pen with markings that disappear when a hot iron is applied to them. The marks can reappear in cold temperatures, however, so you may want to wash your quilt after using this marker.

You can also use marking pens to mark quilting designs on your quilt top. Always test any marking tool before using. To mark straight lines on your quilt top, you can use painter's tape. Just don't leave the tape on for long periods of time, as it may leave a sticky residue. You can also use an air-soluble or water-soluble fabric-marking pen to draw out more complex or free-motion quilting designs. An alternative to a marking pen is a Hera marker; this white plastic tool has a sharp edge that leaves a crease on your fabric rather than ink.

BASTING TOOLS

Basting is the act of securing the three layers of your quilt together to prepare for quilting. For machine quilting, you can utilize basting pins, which are curved safety pins that have an angle designed to easily penetrate all the layers of your quilt. Another option is a basting spray, such as Spray and Fix 505. Basting spray is a temporary, repositionable aerosol fabric adhesive that will hold the layers of your quilt together. For thread basting, you'll need a long needle, such as a darning needle, and white thread.

For additional details on basting, refer to "Preparing for Quilting" on page 83.

More Than You Ever Wanted to Know about Batting

If you visit your local quilt shop or fabric store, you'll find almost as many options for quilt batting as there are varieties of coffee beans! Having so many options can be quite overwhelming. Each different kind of batting serves a purpose and works better in some quilting applications than others. This handy cheat sheet should make batting shopping a breeze.

- **100% cotton.** This type seems to be the most popular among modern quilters, perhaps for its durability. It's a lightweight option that's easy to work with and easy to launder. When the finished quilt is washed, cotton batting creates a crinkly, vintage look, which I personally enjoy very much. All quilts in this book were assembled using Pellon Legacy 100% cotton batting.

- **Poly/cotton blend.** Super smooth to the touch, poly/cotton blended batting is quite popular with machine quilters. It is considered to combine the best parts of both cotton and polyester batting in one package. Quilts with this batting tend to have a slightly thicker look than those with 100% cotton, and a smoother appearance as well, even after washing.

- **100% polyester.** This batting is preferred by some hand quilters because of the ease of needling. Polyester batting has gained a bit of a bad reputation due to bearding, but many polyester products on the market these days are treated to prevent that problem. Polyester batting is a bit warmer than cotton batting, but also more slippery, making it a poor choice for machine quilting.

- **Wool.** Cozy-warm and easy to hand quilt, wool batting is quite popular with hand quilters. Wool has an airy loft that creates highly defined quilting stitches, and it is the warmest type of quilt batting available, but it does require hand washing and may need moth protection if stored.

NICE-TO-HAVE TOOLS

Just as a navigational system isn't an absolute necessity in your car, many of the quilting notions on the market aren't essential for your quiltmaking journey—but they can be very helpful along the way. Here's a quick rundown of some of the more popular and handy extra tools.

An assortment of tools for quilting

Binding clips or Wonder clips. Rather than using straight pins to secure your binding in place when hand sewing it to the back for finishing, you can use binding clips. The binding clips in the photo above look quite a bit like hair barrettes; the Wonder clips look like small clothespins.

Design wall. I positively love my design wall! Mine is simply a large piece of flannel hanging on the wall in my sewing room. The flannel "holds" my cotton quilt blocks in place as I try out various block layouts, and it's also extremely handy for storing works in progress.

Seam ripper. This is a very handy item to have if you've mis-sewn something. Mistakes happen to the best of us. As soon as you notice your seam ripper performing poorly at ripping stitches, or when you notice that ripping is requiring more effort, it's time to replace it. The sharp edge can dull over time.

Specialty rulers and cutting templates. In addition to standard long rulers and square rulers, you'll find many specialty rulers for easy cutting of different shapes. Whether your quiltmaking involves rectangles, squares, circles, triangles, or hexagons, there's a ruler or template to suit your need. These tools can be very helpful for certain cutting tasks—everything from flying geese to Dresden plate blades—but are definitely not necessary. Add to your ruler and template collection judiciously.

Spray starch. To remove stubborn wrinkles from fabric for smooth and accurate cutting, I sometimes use a spritz of Mary Ellen's Best Press spray starch. It's my favorite brand and comes in a nonaerosol spray bottle.

Machine-quilting gloves. Quilting gloves can make your machine-quilting experience much more enjoyable. These lightweight gloves have a gripping surface that helps you use your fingertips to guide the quilt under your machine's needle while free-motion quilting. Manipulating a quilt under your sewing machine can be challenging due to the weight of the quilt top, batting, and backing. Personally, I enjoy using Machingers Quilting Gloves. They are easy to wash and take care of, and they fit me really nicely. I especially like how the grips on the fingertips are flexible and lightweight enough so that I can reload my bobbin without removing my gloves.

ROTARY CUTTING

A rotary cutter makes cutting the fabrics for your quilt much faster and more accurate than cutting with scissors. However, it can be a dangerous tool, so it's important to follow these key safety rules.

- Always cut on a rotary-cutting mat with rulers specifically designed for rotary cutting.

- Cut in a standing position, and cut away from your body.

- Keep your fingers away from the ruler's edge at all times when using the cutter.

- Apply constant pressure to your cutter when cutting, but never press too hard. If you feel yourself constantly having to press harder to get a clean cut, it's time to replace your blade.

- Lock the safety latch whenever the cutter is not in use.

- Dispose of old blades properly and store new ones in a safe place. Rotary-cutter blades usually come in some kind of case for a good reason—to protect you. Leave new blades in the case until you need to put a new one on your cutter. Place the used blade in an empty case before you put it in the trash. Even a dull blade is still quite sharp and can cause harm.

EXERCISE 1
Cutting with Confidence

The activities in this exercise will introduce you to the basics of rotary cutting. Be sure to keep the key safety rules in mind at all times.

Squaring Up Your Fabric

You'll need ½ yard of a fabric of your choosing. The instructions are written for right-handed quilters; if you are left-handed, reverse the placement of the ruler and rotary cutter throughout the steps.

1 Press your fabric well to eliminate any wrinkles or creases from folding.

2 Fold the fabric along its length, with the selvages aligned. Your cut edges may not line up; don't worry, this is OK! The fold should have no puckers or wrinkles and should allow the selvages to match up.

3 Place your fabric on your cutting mat, with the fold in the fabric closest to you. An 18" x 24" mat should accommodate the fabric, but if your mat is smaller, you will need to make a second fold to fit the fabric on your mat. Keep in mind that the more folds you make, the greater the chance for inaccuracy. Don't worry about the grid lines on your mat; we won't be using those for this exercise. You can even use the plain side of your mat if you prefer.

4 Place your 6" x 24" ruler over the fabric, aligning the 1" line of your ruler with the fabric fold. Hold the ruler firmly in place with your left hand. Keeping the horizontal line of the ruler aligned with the fold, use your rotary cutter to cut off a skinny strip of fabric. Make sure that you cut through both layers along the length of the fabric. Your fabric is now officially squared up! Leave the fabric in place on the cutting mat.

Discard.

Cutting Strips and Squares

Once your fabric is squared up, you can move on to cutting strips along the width of the fabric and subcutting squares or rectangles from your strips. In this part of the exercise we'll cut a 5"-wide strip and subcut it into a few squares and rectangles.

1 After squaring up your fabric, rotate your cutting mat 180° to position the selvage edges closest to you and the fold away from you. By rotating the mat, you avoid disturbing the cut edges of the fabric. The edges from your square-up cut will now be on the left side.

2 Place your 6" x 24" ruler over the fabric, aligning the 5" line on the ruler with the straight edge you just cut. Hold the ruler firmly in place with your left hand and cut along the right side of the ruler with the rotary cutter. You'll now have a folded 5"-wide strip of fabric that is approximately 42" long (the width of your fabric).

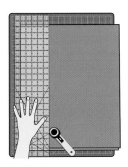

3 Fold and set aside the bulk of the fabric. We'll work with the 5" strip for the remainder of this exercise. Keep the strip folded with raw edges even.

4 Cut off the selvage edges by placing your ruler on the strip and aligning it with the cut edges of the fabric. Cut off about 1", which includes the selvages. This gives you a clean cut, perpendicular to the long edges.

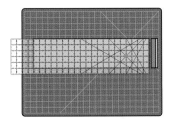

5 To cut a square, rotate the mat 180°. Align the 5" line of your ruler with the newly cut end of your strip. Cut along the edge of the ruler. Ta-da! You have just cut two identical 5" squares from your fabric. This process can be repeated to cut as many additional squares as you need.

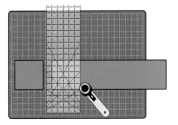

6 To cut rectangles, simply align the desired measurement with the newly cut end of the strip. For 2½" x 5" rectangles, place the 2½" line along the cut edge and rotary cut along the edge of the ruler. You'll have two rectangles. Now you've learned the basics of rotary cutting. Pat yourself on the back!

Why Square Up Your Fabric?

Squaring up the fabric allows you to make accurate cuts along the grain of the fabric, preventing the fabric from stretching when it's not supposed to.

If you're wondering what *grain* is, take a close look at your fabric. Quilting fabric is made up of tons of fine lengths of thread, woven together at 90° angles. These threads form the grain of the fabric. The longest threads run parallel to the selvage edges. This is referred to as the *lengthwise* grain. Shorter threads run from selvage to selvage. This is the *crosswise* grain. When you cut fabric on the grain, the fabric will have less stretch to it and will perform best in a quilt. Lengthwise grain has the least stretch. Fabric cut off-grain (on the bias) will stretch easily and can result in inaccurate piecing. Cut off-grain *only* when instructed. In some cases, you want the fabric to stretch, as in curved piecing or when binding curved edges. But for most piecing, cutting on the straight of grain is best.

PIECING BASICS

Most, if not all, piecing in quiltmaking is based upon the use of a scant ¼" seam allowance. This seam allowance, when sewn accurately, will allow you to follow any quilt pattern or tutorial and produce results in the size stated in the pattern. With the exception of improvisational piecing or paper foundation piecing, a consistent scant ¼" seam is key for quilting.

What's a Seam Allowance?

A seam allowance is the area between your line of stitching and the raw edges of the fabric. The seam hides the raw edges under your piecing.

WHAT IS A SCANT ¼" SEAM?

Sewing a scant ¼" seam is not the same as simply stitching ¼" from the raw edges of your fabric. When you press seam allowances, even when you press them open, you'll lose some fabric in the seam. Stitching a scant ¼" seam—a couple of threads closer to the raw edge of your fabric—allows you to lose exactly ¼" from each of the fabrics you're sewing together. A couple of threads may not sound like much, but they multiply quickly across an entire quilt.

For my first few quilts, my seam allowance was anything but a scant ¼", as I hadn't yet understood or mastered that. My quilts always finished a tad smaller than the pattern specified. Because my seams were consistent, the blocks still lined up correctly. That's not always the case, however; many blocks do indeed depend on that scant ¼" seam allowance in order for each part of the block to fit together and line up correctly.

Another reason to strive for the perfect scant ¼" is that if you work with others on a group quilt, the blocks won't fit together correctly if the seam allowances aren't consistent. It's important as a quilter to produce a scant ¼" seam consistently throughout your projects.

You can set up your sewing machine several ways to help you produce a consistent, scant ¼"-wide seam allowance. For many sewing machines, a special foot, called a ¼" quilting foot, is available from your dealer. This foot is usually set up with a metal or plastic guide with which to line up the raw edges of fabric while sewing. But this foot alone will not necessarily guarantee a scant ¼" seam—you may have to adjust the position of your fabric as you feed it through, or move your needle position to actually produce the seam allowance you're after.

Right Sides Together

Always sew with right sides together—unless instructed otherwise. The seam allowances will then be on the wrong sides of the fabric, the wrong sides of a block, and on the wrong side of a quilt top. Some fabrics, such as solids, don't have a right or wrong side, but other fabrics have only subtle differences between the right and wrong sides, so you may need to take extra care when piecing if that is the case.

CHAIN PIECING

I positively adore chain piecing. I like to call it assembly-line piecing, because that's precisely what it is. Once all of the cutting is complete, you sew pieces together one pair at a time, feeding them through your sewing machine one right after another, without trimming the threads between each pair. This creates a chain of patchwork. When you're finished, clip the threads holding your patches together and press. This method saves time and thread.

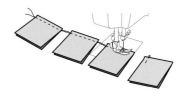

EXERCISE ❷
Finding the Sweet Spot for Your Scant ¼" Seam

This exercise will help you set up your sewing machine for a precise quilting seam allowance.

1 Attach a ¼" quilting foot if you have one, or use your standard presser foot.

2 Cut two 2½" x 2½" squares of any 100% cotton fabric.

3 Layer the two squares right sides together, lining up the raw edges, and stitch along one side using the edge of the presser foot as a guide.

4 Finger-press the seam open, and then press with a hot, dry iron. (See "Exercise 3" on page 18.)

5 Grab a ruler and measure your patchwork—it should now measure exactly 4½" wide. Does it? If so, great job! You're all set up to sew a scant ¼" seam allowance.

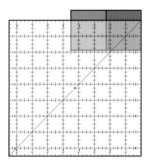

If the piece is not 4½" wide, take a closer look. Is the seam straight, or a bit irregular? If the seam is a bit wobbly, try again. Sew slowly to see if that will improve your accuracy.

Are the raw edges of fabric still aligned? If they slipped while stitching, try pressing the squares together with a hot iron before sewing. That may help them stick better and prevent shifting.

If your seam is straight and your raw edges are aligned, it's time to move your needle position. Move the needle slightly to the right if you need to shrink the seam allowance; alternatively, move the needle position to the left if you need to increase the seam allowance. Refer to your sewing machine's manual for instructions on needle positioning.

Find the Sweet Spot

If your sewing machine is equipped with a straight stitch plate with a single hole for the needle to pass through, you won't be able to adjust the needle position. Instead, use the tape method discussed below to find the sweet spot for a scant ¼" seam allowance.

Once you've moved your needle position, cut two more 2½" x 2½" squares and repeat the exercise. Press and measure. If your seam is now accurate, I suggest jotting down the needle position and taping it to the side of your sewing machine so that you won't forget in the future. If your seam is still inaccurate, you may want to visit your local quilt shop or sewing-machine dealer to purchase a seam guide that can help you align your fabric pieces for accuracy.

If you're unable to move the needle on your machine, you can use quilter's masking tape or painter's tape to make a guide on the bed of your sewing machine. Measure ¼" from the needle and place a line of tape, being sure not to cover the feed dogs. You'll line up the raw edges of your fabric with the edge of the tape. Repeat the exercise and reposition the tape until you are good to go. Add a couple more layers of tape and you'll have a perfect ¼" seam guide.

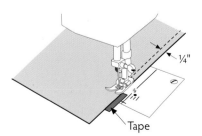

Tape

PRESSING

When using an iron during the quilting process, there's a big difference between *pressing* and *ironing*. Pressing is a gentle lifting and setting-down motion. Ironing is moving the iron across your fabric with pressure, as when you iron a shirt. Ironing can actually distort your piecing by stretching your fabric. Pressing, on the other hand, flattens the patchwork that has been stitched and helps you to join pieces accurately.

PRESS OPEN OR TO THE SIDE?

Quilters are divided about the preferred direction for pressing seam allowances. Many press them to the side; I choose to press them open. When seams are pressed open, you spread the bulk of your seams throughout the quilt. I find that this creates flatter blocks and a smoother quilt top, which then makes quilting easier. There are situations, such as foundation piecing, when pressing to the side is a necessity, but aside from that, my seam allowances are always pressed open. I sew with a shorter than average stitch length when pressing seams open, setting my machine at 2.0 mm rather than 2.5 mm.

Pressing to the side harkens back to the days when our great-grandmothers pieced their quilts by hand, and pressing to the side gave the quilt additional structural integrity. If you've always been a side presser, give open pressing a try and see what you think. I bet you'll find that open pressing gives your finished quilts a beautifully smooth look.

Pressed to one side. Pressed open.

WHAT ABOUT STARCH?

I rarely use regular starch in my quilting, although I do use Mary Ellen's Best Press on occasion to get stubborn wrinkles out of new fabric. Best Press comes in a spray bottle rather than an aerosol can, and it has a softer feel than most starch products. Experiment to find what works best for you.

EXERCISE ❸
Pressing 101

1 While the iron heats up, finger-press your seam allowances open on your patchwork created in "Exercise 2" on page 17. Run your fingernail along the seam, opening it up.

2 Lay the patchwork wrong side up. Place the iron on the seam, pressing gently, and then lift the iron after about three seconds.

3 Allow your patchwork to cool briefly before removing it from the ironing board.

Pressing Tips

- Use a dry iron. This will improve your accuracy, as steam can distort your seams.

- Press often. Press your fabric before cutting and press again as you piece to lock your seams in place.

- Using a fabric other than 100% cotton in your project? Test a small piece with your iron to make sure it doesn't scorch. Adjust your heat setting as needed.

- Remove pins before pressing. Just because they're heatproof doesn't mean you should iron over them.

- Use the tip of the iron to open up stubborn seams.

- So that you don't singe your fingers while pressing your seams open, finger-press the seams first, before picking up the iron. Then press the patchwork with a hot iron.

14 PATTERNS TO BUILD YOUR QUILTING SKILLS

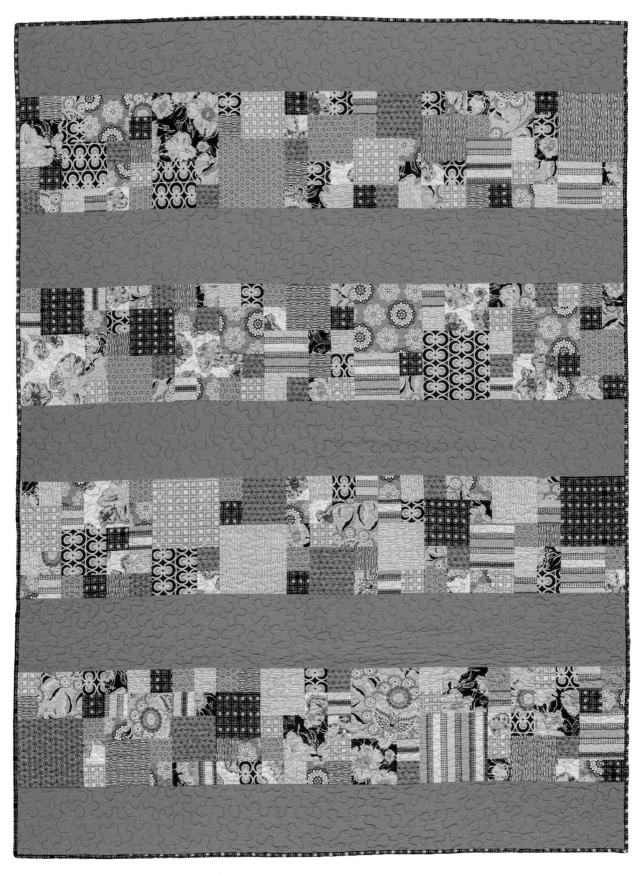

Finished quilt: 54" x 70"   **Finished block:** 10" x 18"
Fabrics from various collections for Art Gallery Fabrics

PATCHWORK DREAMS

*S*imple squares in varying sizes create an interesting rectangular patchwork block. The block is repeated in rows separated by swaths of brightly colored sashing. This is a great pattern for your first quilt, allowing you plenty of practice sewing your scant ¼" seam. As you select fabrics, keep in mind that each fat quarter will be cut into both large squares and small ones. Some large prints may lose a bit of their appeal when cut into 2½" squares, while others can work well. See the box below for tips on auditioning prints.

MATERIALS

Yardage is based on 42"-wide fabric.

12 fat quarters of assorted prints for patchwork

1½ yards of emerald solid for sashing

⅝ yard of small-scale print for binding

3½ yards of fabric for backing

62" x 78" piece of batting

Auditioning Prints

Some large-scale prints work quite well when cut into small pieces. An easy way to get a feel for this is by covering the fabric with your hands, leaving just a 2" or 2½" square open between your thumbs and forefingers. This lets you see the visual impression made by a small area of the print. You can also cut an opening in a blank piece of paper and move it around on the fabric.

CUTTING

From *each* of the 12 fat quarters, cut:
 1 square, 6½" x 6½"
 4 squares, 4½" x 4½"
 20 squares, 2½" x 2½"

From the emerald solid, cut:
 7 strips, 6½" x 42"

From the binding fabric, cut:
 7 strips, 2½" x 42"

If Bigger Is Better

Have your heart set on a queen-size quilt? You'll need to make 30 blocks, set 5 x 6, for a 90" x 102½" finished size.

Materials

30 fat quarters of assorted prints for patchwork

3½ yards of solid for sashing

⅞ yard of fabric for binding

8½ yards of fabric for backing

98" x 110" piece of batting

PIECING THE BLOCKS

This block is pieced in columns. For each block you will need 20 print 2½" squares, four print 4½" squares, and one print 6½" square. Be sure to select a variety of prints for each block. Use a scant ¼" seam allowance and press seam allowances open after sewing each seam.

1 To make the left column, sew six print 2½" squares together into three pairs. Sew one pair to the top edge of a print 4½" square. Sew the two remaining pairs together to create a four-patch unit. Sew the four-patch unit to the bottom of the 4½" square.

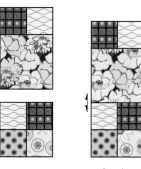

Left column

2 For the center column, sew 12 print 2½" squares together into six pairs. Sew one pair to each side of a print 4½" square. Sew two pairs together to create a four-patch unit. Sew this unit to the right side of another print 4½" square. Sew two pairs of squares together to create a chain of four squares. Assemble the units into a column.

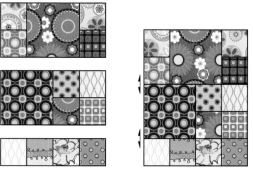

Center column

3 For the right column, sew two print 2½" squares together. Sew this pair to the right side of a print 4½" square. Sew this unit to the bottom of a print 6½" square.

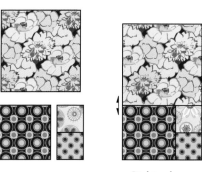

Right column

4 Sew the left and center columns together, and then add the right column.

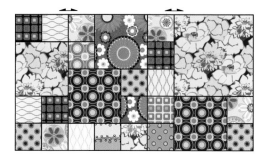

5 Repeat steps 1–4 to make a total of 12 blocks.

Don't Be Afraid of Color

Experiment with color! When you go fabric shopping, put colors together that you wouldn't normally think of. That's how the sashing for this quilt wound up being emerald. I initially wanted to use a purple or a light sea green for the sashing, because I felt it would best complement the colors of my fat quarters. Ultimately, though, I went for a bold emerald green, and I'm extremely pleased with how well it accents my prints.

ASSEMBLING THE QUILT TOP

1 Arrange your blocks into four rows of three blocks each in an order that is pleasing to your eye. I rotated every other block to create more movement and variety in the quilt. Once you're happy with the layout, sew the blocks in each row together, pressing seam allowances open as you go.

2 Join the seven 6½" x 42" emerald strips together to make one long strip. Press the seam allowances open. Cut into five lengths, 6½" x 54½", for the sashing rows.

3 Sew the sashing rows together with the block rows, alternating them as shown in the quilt assembly diagram. Press.

FINISHING THE QUILT

1 Piece the backing together using a horizontal seam. The backing should measure at least 62" x 78".

2 Baste, quilt as desired, and bind. For more details, see "Finishing Your Quilts" on page 81.

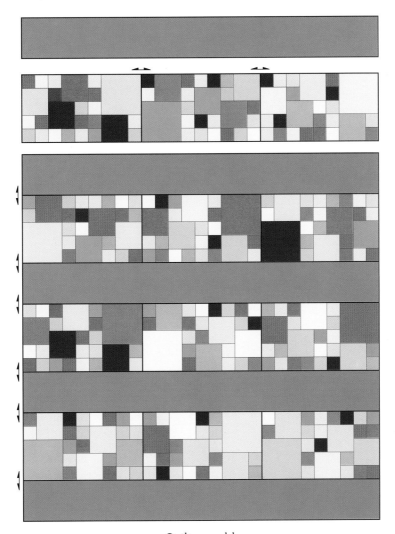

Quilt assembly

Finished quilt: 60" x 70"   **Finished block:** 10" x 10"
Fabrics from Rashida Coleman-Hale's Washi collection for Timeless Treasures Fabrics

PRECIOUS STONES

*T*his quilt uses one of my favorite kinds of patchwork: a maze-style design. The patchwork squares create the look of an interlocking maze across the quilt, inviting you to really have fun with your fabric selections. You can use lots of variety, both in the scale of your prints and with colors; or, you might substitute jewel-toned solids as a great alternative to prints. I used a neutral background fabric, but you could easily use a subtle print that contrasts well with the other fabrics. This is another good chance for you to build your skills with rotary cutting and sewing the perfect scant ¼" seam.

MATERIALS

Yardage is based on 42"-wide fabric.

14 fat quarters of assorted prints for blocks

2¼ yards of white fabric for background

⅝ yard of medium-scale print for binding

3⅞ yards of fabric for backing

68" x 78" piece of batting

If Bigger Is Better

If you prefer a queen-size version of this quilt, you'll need to make 90 blocks, set 9 x 10, for a 90" x 102½" finished size.

Materials

30 fat quarters of assorted prints for blocks

5 yards of white fabric for background

⅞ yard of fabric for binding

8½ yards of fabric for backing

98" x 111" piece of batting

CUTTING

From *each* of the 14 fat quarters, cut:
   42 squares, 2½" x 2½"

From the white fabric, cut:
   29 strips, 2½" x 42"; crosscut into:
      126 squares, 2½" x 2½"
      84 rectangles, 2½" x 8½"

From the binding fabric, cut:
   7 strips, 2½" x 42"

PIECING THE BLOCKS

Use a scant ¼" seam allowance and press seam allowances open after sewing each seam.

1 Sew three 2½" squares of assorted prints together into a column. Make 126 of these three-square units, chain piecing them for efficiency.

Make 126.

2 Sew a white 2½" square to each of the three-square units from step 1.

Make 126.

3 Sew three units from step 2 and two white 2½" x 8½" rectangles together, orienting the units from step 2 as shown. Make 42.

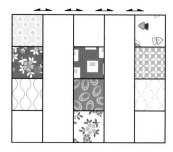

Make 42.

4 Sew five 2½" squares of assorted prints together to create a horizontal patchwork strip. Sew the strip to the top of a unit from step 3. Repeat to make a total of 42 blocks.

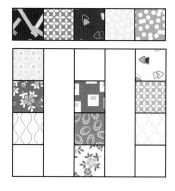

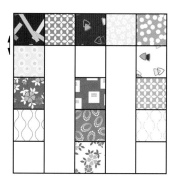

Make 42.

ASSEMBLING THE QUILT TOP

1 Arrange your blocks into seven rows of six blocks each in an order that is pleasing to your eye. Once you're happy with the layout, sew the blocks in each row together, pressing seam allowances open as you go.

2 Sew the rows together to complete the quilt top. I like to sew the rows together in pairs first and then sew the pairs together. Press.

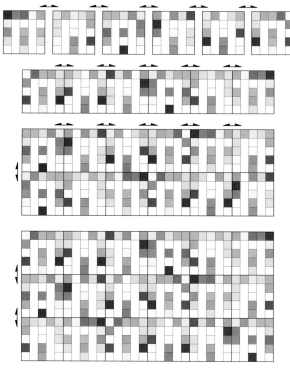

Quilt assembly

FINISHING THE QUILT

1 Piece the backing together using a horizontal seam. The backing should measure at least 68" x 78".

2 Baste, quilt as desired, and bind. For more details, see "Finishing Your Quilts" on page 81.

SOPHISTICATED SQUARE

*T*his cheery square project is perfect as a play mat or cuddly quilt for a baby or toddler, or even as a wall hanging to show off some of your favorite fabrics. Take your time with fabric selection, keeping in mind that the frame fabrics that create the borders will finish at 2" wide. Large-scale prints can work in this quilt, but they will look quite different when cut into narrow strips. I chose a large-scale striped fabric for the center square. It gives the illusion of being strip pieced without the work. Have fun choosing your background fabric as well—a bright, vibrant color would give your quilt a truly funky look!

MATERIALS

Yardage is based on 42"-wide fabric.

2 yards of white solid for background

⅝ yard of focus fabric for center square and pieced border

⅝ yard of blue print for frame 3 and pieced border

½ yard of orange print for frame 1 and pieced border

½ yard of multicolored print for frame 2 and pieced border

⅝ yard of yellow print for binding

3⅔ yards of fabric for backing

66" x 66" piece of batting

CUTTING

From the focus fabric, cut:
1 square, 18½" x 18½"
13 rectangles, 2½" x 6½"

From the orange print, cut:
2 strips, 2½" x 22½"
2 strips, 2½" x 26½"
12 rectangles, 2½" x 6½"

From the multicolored print, cut:
2 strips, 2½" x 30½"
2 strips, 2½" x 34½"
13 rectangles, 2½" x 6½"

From the blue print, cut:
2 strips, 2½" x 38½"
2 strips, 2½" x 42½"
12 rectangles, 2½" x 6½"

From the white solid, *cut on the lengthwise grain*:
2 strips, 2½" x 18½"
2 strips, 2½" x 22½"
2 strips, 2½" x 26½"
2 strips, 2½" x 30½"
2 strips, 2½" x 34½"
2 strips, 2½" x 38½"
2 strips, 2½" x 42½"
2 strips, 2½" x 46½"
54 rectangles, 2½" x 6½"

From the binding fabric, cut:
7 strips, 2½" x 42"

Go Scrappy!

This quilt is a play on a traditional Log Cabin quilt, and is ripe for reinterpretation. Instead of using one focus fabric and three coordinating prints, try using several. You could even utilize a different fabric for every strip. Have fun with it! If you look closely at the outer border, you'll notice that I threw in some additional coordinating prints when cutting and piecing that final border.

Finished quilt: 58" x 58"

Fabrics from Thomas Knauer's Flock collection for Andover Fabrics

PIECING THE QUILT TOP

Use a scant ¼" seam allowance and press seam allowances open after sewing each seam.

1 Sew the white 2½" x 18½" strips to the top and bottom of the 18½" square of focus fabric. Sew the white 2½" x 22½" strips to the left and right sides.

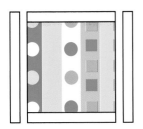 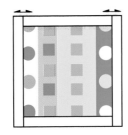

2 Referring to the diagram below, sew the orange-print 2½" x 22½" strips to the top and bottom of the center unit. Sew the orange-print 2½" x 26½" strips to the left and right sides.

3 Sew the white 2½" x 26½" strips to the top and bottom of the center unit. Sew the white 2½" x 30½" strips to the left and right sides.

4 Sew the multicolored 2½" x 30½" strips to the top and bottom of the center unit. Sew the multicolored 2½" x 34½" strips to the left and right sides.

5 Sew the white 2½" x 34½" strips to the top and bottom of the center unit. Sew the white 2½" x 38½" strips to the left and right sides.

6 Sew the blue-print 2½" x 38½" strips to the top and bottom of the center unit. Sew the blue-print 2½" x 42½" strips to the left and right sides.

7 Sew the white 2½" x 42½" strips to the top and bottom of the center unit. Sew the white 2½" x 46½" strips to the left and right sides.

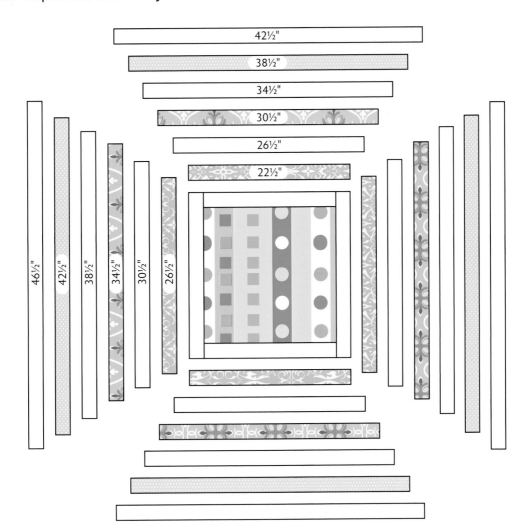

8 To create the pieced borders, join 12 white 2½" x 6½" rectangles and 11 print 2½" x 6½" rectangles, alternating them as shown. Make two. Join 15 white 2½" x 6½" rectangles and 14 print 2½" x 6½" rectangles in the same manner. Make two.

Make 2.

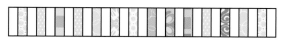

Make 2.

9 Sew the shorter border strips to the top and bottom of the quilt center. Press the seam allowances open. Add the longer strips to the sides. Press the seam allowances open.

FINISHING THE QUILT

1 Piece the backing together using a horizontal or vertical seam. The backing should measure at least 66" x 66".

2 Baste, quilt as desired, and bind. For more details, see "Finishing Your Quilts" on page 81.

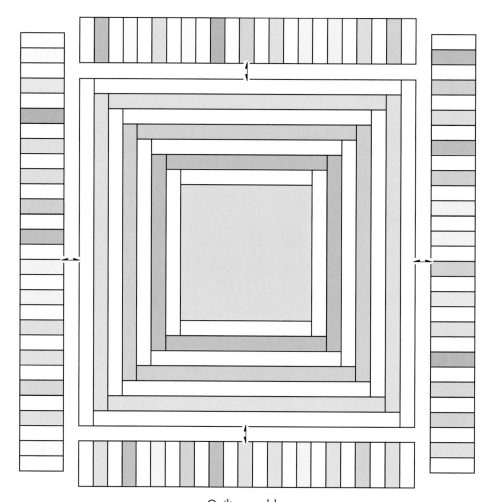

Quilt assembly

LESS IS MORE

I love working with solids, and this quilt is an expression of that love. Using three different values of four of my favorite colors, I created simple patchwork blocks that are set on point and bordered by lots of negative space to let the jewel tones really shine. I love how using solids in a quilt can really emphasize the design of the pattern or block you're working with. Using solids accentuates the geometric shapes in quilts, and it's a lot of fun to add texture with your quilting stitches. For a unique twist, you could use tone-on-tone or tone-and-white prints rather than solids for the blocks.

MATERIALS

Yardage is based on 42"-wide fabric.

3½ yards of gray solid for blocks, setting triangles, and borders

1 fat quarter each of dark-value red, purple, blue, and green solids for blocks

1 fat quarter each of light-value red*, purple, blue, and green solids for blocks

1 fat eighth each of medium-value red*, purple, blue, and green solids for blocks

⅝ yard of dark-gray solid for binding

3¾ yards of fabric for backing

64" x 78" piece of batting

*Note that there is a very subtle difference between the light red and medium red that I used in my blocks. Feel free to choose fabrics with greater or lesser value differences.

CUTTING

From each dark solid of red, purple, and blue, cut:
6 squares, 2¾" x 2¾"
6 rectangles, 2¾" x 5"

From the dark-green solid, cut:
4 squares, 2¾" x 2¾"
4 rectangles, 2¾" x 5"

From each medium solid of red, purple, and blue, cut:
3 squares, 2¾" x 2¾"

From the medium-green solid, cut:
2 squares, 2¾" x 2¾"

From each light solid of red, purple, and blue, cut:
6 squares, 2¾" x 2¾"
6 rectangles, 2¾" x 5"

From the light-green solid, cut:
4 squares, 2¾" x 2¾"
4 rectangles, 2¾" x 5"

From the gray solid, cut on the lengthwise grain:
1 strip, 15" x 70½"
1 strip, 10½" x 70½"
2 strips, 3½" x 32½"

From the remainder of the gray solid, cut:
9 strips, 2¾" x 42"; crosscut into:
  44 rectangles, 2¾" x 5"
  44 squares, 2¾" x 2¾"
2 squares, 17¼" x 17¼"; cut into quarters diagonally to yield 8 triangles
2 squares, 8⅞" x 8⅞"; cut in half diagonally to yield 4 triangles

From the binding fabric, cut:
7 strips, 2½" x 42"

Finished quilt: 56½" x 70"   **Finished block:** 11¼" x 11¼"

Fabrics from the Free Spirit Designer Solids collection for Free Spirit Fabrics

PIECING THE BLOCKS

Use a scant ¼" seam allowance and press seam allowances open after sewing each seam.

1 Pair a dark solid 2¾" square with a gray 2¾" square and sew them together. Make 22. Pair the remaining gray 2¾" squares with the light solid 2¾" squares and sew them together. Make 22.

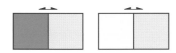

Make 22 of each.

2 Sew a matching dark 2¾" x 5" rectangle to each of the dark units from step 1 as shown. Sew a matching light 2¾" x 5" rectangle to each of the light units from step 1.

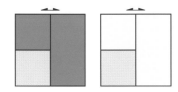

Make 22 of each.

3 Sew two gray 2¾" x 5" rectangles to opposite sides of each medium 2¾" square. Make 11 for the block centers.

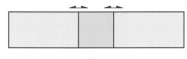

Make 11.

4 Arrange two gray 2¾" x 5" rectangles, two matching dark and two matching light units from step 2, and a corresponding unit from step 3

as shown. Sew the units into rows and press. Sew the rows together to complete the block. Repeat to make three blocks each of red, blue, and purple and two green blocks.

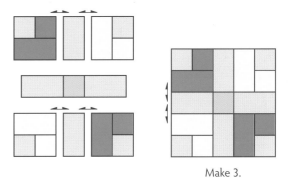

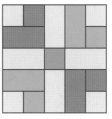

Make 3.

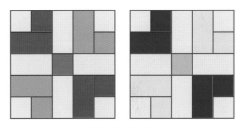

Make 3 of each.

Make 2.

ASSEMBLING THE QUILT TOP

1 Arrange your blocks into diagonal rows as shown. To complete the sides of the quilt, you'll need to add setting triangles. Position the gray quarter-square setting triangles along the sides, and add the half-square setting triangles to the corners. Sew the pieces together into rows, pressing seam allowances open as you go.

2 Sew the rows together. Press.

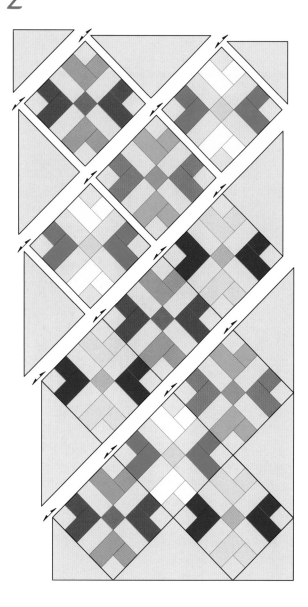

3 Sew the gray 3½" x 32½" strips to the top and bottom of the quilt center. Press seam allowances open. Sew the gray 10½" x 70½" strip to the right side of the quilt center, and add the gray 15" x 70½" strip to the left side. Press.

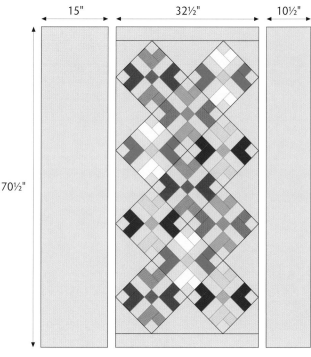

Quilt assembly

FINISHING THE QUILT

1 Piece the backing together using a horizontal seam. The backing should measure at least 64" x 78".

2 Baste, quilt as desired, and bind. For more details, see "Finishing Your Quilts" on page 81.

MONTEREY SQUARE

*T*his was the first quilt I worked on for this book, and I felt it needed an important name. I named it after one of the squares in Savannah, Georgia, where my husband and I spent our honeymoon. Monterey Square is especially picturesque and home to Mercer House, featured heavily in John Berendt's book Midnight in the Garden of Good and Evil. This quilt and the way the squares are connected throughout makes me think of the layout of the city of Savannah—a grid of squares connected by various streets.

This pattern is fabulous for using big, bold prints. Large-scale florals and paisleys are easy to fall in love with at the quilt shop, but they can be difficult to use when cut into tiny pieces for quilts. In this design, you'll be able to showcase your favorite prints by pairing them up with coordinating solids. You'll also have the chance to use a favorite print or solid in the parallel lines that run the length of the quilt—and increase your rotary-cutting confidence at the same time.

MATERIALS

Yardage is based on 42"-wide fabric.

10 fat quarters of assorted large-scale prints for blocks*

⅜ yard *each* of 5 coordinating solids for blocks

1⅜ yards of white solid for sashing

1⅛ yards of small- or medium-scale print for vertical strips**

⅔ yard of print for binding

4⅔ yards of fabric for backing

72" x 84" piece of batting

*You can also use 30 precut squares, 10" x 10".

**A coordinating solid would work well here too.

CUTTING

Refer to the cutting diagram on page 37 when cutting the fat quarters.

From *each* of the 10 fat quarters, cut:
    3 rectangles, 8½" x 9½"

From *each* of the 5 coordinating solids, cut:
    12 rectangles, 1½" x 8½"
    12 rectangles, 1½" x 11"

If Bigger Is Better

Are you planning to make a queen-size quilt? Make 56 blocks, set 7 x 8, for an 89" x 101" finished size.

Materials

19 fat quarters of assorted large-scale prints for blocks

½ yard *each* of 7 coordinating solids for blocks

2⅓ yards of white solid for sashing

2¼ yards of small- or medium-scale print or solid for vertical strips

⅞ yard of print for binding

8 yards of fabric for backing

97" x 110" piece of batting

Continued on page 37

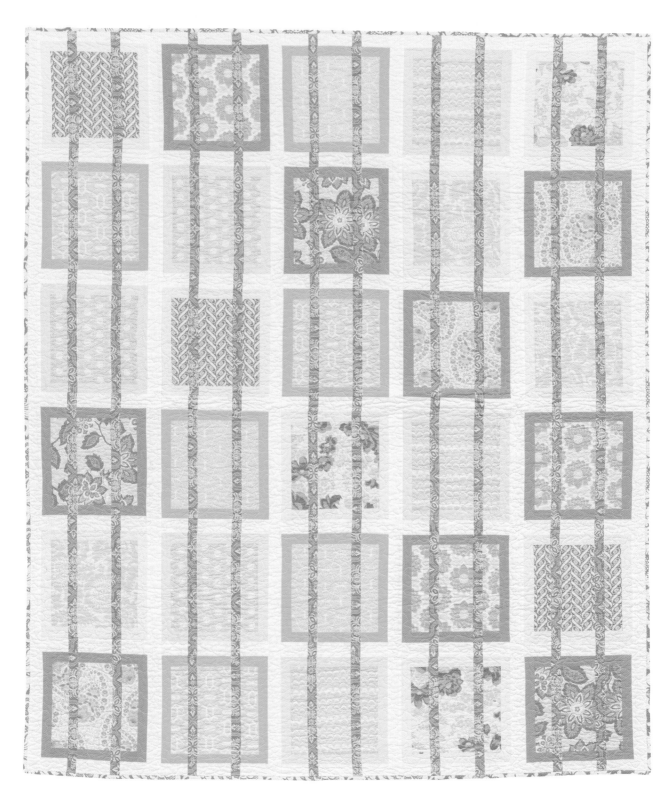

Finished quilt: 64" x 76½"   **Finished block:** 11" x 11"
Fabrics from Joel Dewberry's Heirloom collection for Free Spirit Fabrics, as well as Kona solids

From the small- or medium-scale print, cut:
  24 strips, 1½" x 42"; crosscut into:
    70 rectangles, 1½" x 2"
    60 rectangles, 1½" x 11½"

From the white solid, cut:
  22 strips, 2" x 42"; crosscut 10 strips into:
    70 rectangles, 2" x 3¼"
    35 rectangles, 2" x 4"

From the binding fabric, cut:
  8 strips, 2½" x 42"

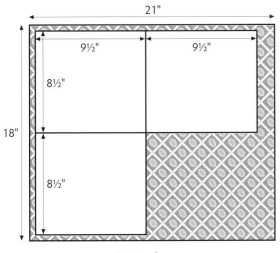

Cutting diagram

PIECING THE BLOCKS

Use a scant ¼" seam allowance and press seam allowances open after sewing each seam.

1 Match up the print 8½" x 9½" rectangles with the solid rectangles in your desired color combinations.

2 Sew a solid 1½" x 8½" rectangle to each 8½"-long side of a large-scale print rectangle. Sew matching solid 1½" x 11" rectangles to the top and bottom of the unit. Press.

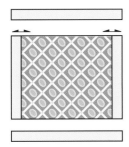
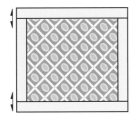

3 Place the block from step 2 on your cutting mat, rotating it so that the shorter side is closest to you. Using your ruler, measure 3¼" from the left side of the block, and make a vertical cut along that line.

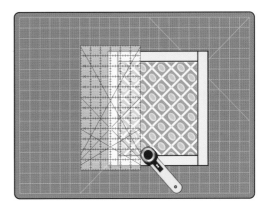

4 Rotate the cutting mat 180° and measure 3¼" from the opposite side of the block. Make a second vertical cut along that line. You now have three sections for your block.

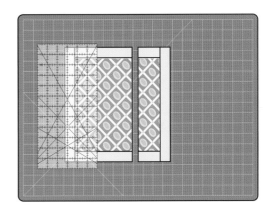

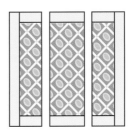

5 Place the small- or medium-scale print 1½" x 11½" rectangles between the sections and sew them together as shown. Press the seam allowances open. The block should measure 11½" x 11½".

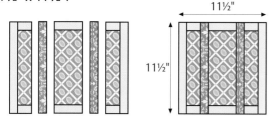

6 Repeat steps 2–5 to make a total of 30 blocks.

You Can Do It!

The first time you cut into a constructed block can be awfully nerve-racking—what if I cut wrong? Cut with *confidence*. Measure twice, and cut once. Cut firmly, while holding your ruler in place, as described in "Exercise 1: Cutting with Confidence" on page 14.

ASSEMBLING THE QUILT TOP

You'll piece this quilt top in columns rather than rows. Pieced horizontal sashing strips go between the blocks, and unpieced sashing strips go between the columns.

1 To make the pieced sashing strip, sew a print 1½" x 2" rectangle to each end of a white 2" x 4" rectangle, matching up the 2"-long raw edges. Press the seam allowances open. Sew a white 2" x 3¼" rectangle to each end of the unit as shown. Make 35.

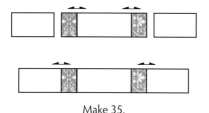

Make 35.

2 Arrange the 30 blocks into five columns of six blocks each in an order that is pleasing to your eye. You can arrange the blocks with the same solid together, or distribute them throughout the quilt top. I placed my blocks randomly throughout the quilt. Place a pieced sashing strip between the blocks in each column and at the top and bottom of the columns.

3 Working with one column at a time, sew the sashing pieces and blocks together, taking care to match up the seams of the print fabrics to create the illusion that one piece of fabric runs the length of the quilt. Press seam allowances open. The columns should measure 76½" in length. Make five columns.

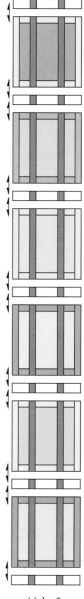

Make 5.

4 Piece the 12 white 2" x 42" strips together in pairs for the vertical sashing. Cut each sewn pair to measure 2" x 76½". Sew the block columns and sashing strips together as shown. Press the seam allowances open.

FINISHING THE QUILT

1 Piece the backing together using a vertical seam. The backing should measure at least 72" x 84".

2 Baste, quilt as desired, and bind. For more details, see "Finishing Your Quilts" on page 81.

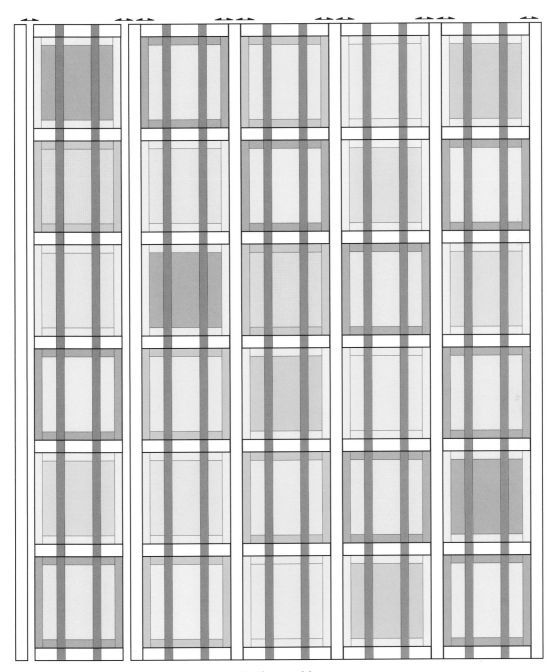

Quilt assembly

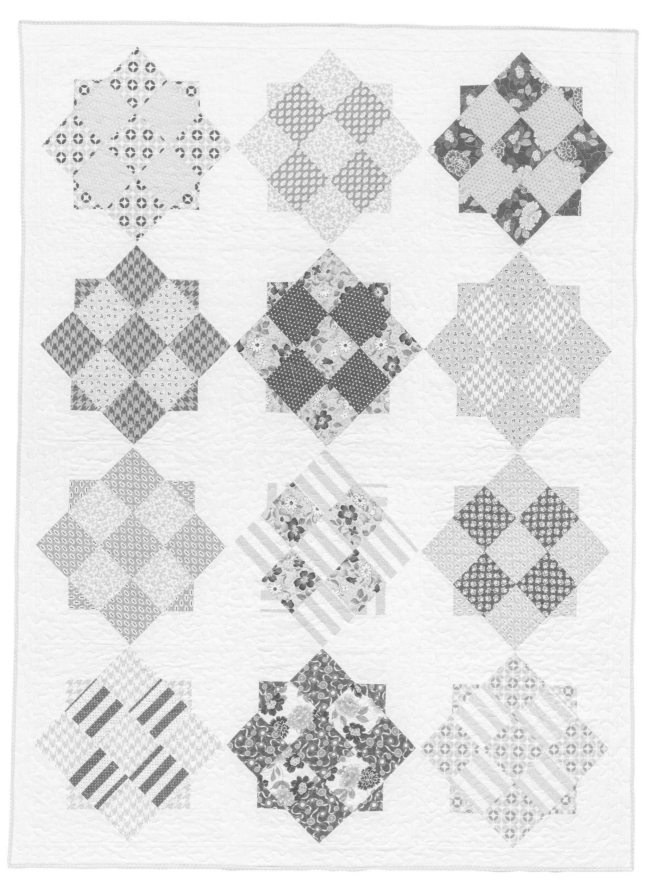

Finished quilt: 55" x 72"   **Finished block:** 17" x 17"
Fabrics from Bonnie & Camille's Vintage Modern collection for Moda Fabrics

REFRESHINGLY RETRO

*H*ere's a fun twist on the simple Nine Patch, a classic block that has remained popular throughout quilting history. Nine Patch blocks consist of nine equal-sized squares, often featuring just two fabrics with a great deal of contrast in color or value. This quilt builds on the principle of the two-color Nine Patch, but it turns the blocks on point and frames them with pieced setting triangles. When working with triangles, keep in mind that you're working with bias edges. Bias seams will have some stretch to them, so handle the fabrics with care or you may wind up with distortion in your finished blocks.

MATERIALS

Yardage is based on 42"-wide fabric.

1 fat quarter or ¼ yard *each* of 12 assorted prints for blocks

1 fat eighth *each* of 12 assorted prints for blocks

2⅜ yards of white solid for blocks and border

⅝ yard of small-scale print for binding

3¾ yards of fabric for backing

63" x 80" piece of batting

If Bigger Is Better

To make a queen-size quilt, you'll need to make 30 blocks, set 5 x 6, for an 89" x 106" finished size.

Materials

1 fat quarter or ¼ yard *each* of 30 assorted prints for blocks

1 fat eighth *each* of 30 assorted prints for blocks

3¼ yards of background fabric for blocks and border

1 yard of fabric for binding

8½ yards of fabric for backing

97" x 114" piece of batting

CUTTING

From *each* of the 12 fat quarters or ¼-yard pieces, cut:
    5 squares, 4½" x 4½"
    2 squares, 3½" x 3½"

From *each* of the 12 fat eighths, cut:
    4 squares, 4½" x 4½"

From the white solid, *cut on the lengthwise grain*:
    2 strips, 2½" x 51½"
    2 strips, 2½" x 72½"

From the remainder of the white solid, cut:
    48 squares, 3½" x 3½"
    48 rectangles, 3½" x 9½"

From the binding fabric, cut:
    7 strips, 2½" x 42"

PIECING THE BLOCKS

Use a scant ¼" seam allowance and press seam allowances open after sewing each seam.

1 Select two matching print 3½" squares and sew a white 3½" square to the top and bottom of each. Sew a white 3½" x 9½" rectangle to each side. Make two.

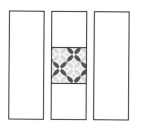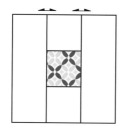

Make 2.

2 Place the pieced square on your cutting mat. Using your ruler and rotary cutter, cut the block in half diagonally, from corner to corner, creating two setting triangles. Repeat for the second block to make four triangles.

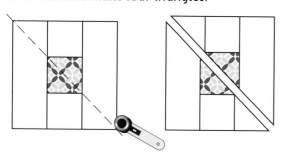

3 Choose four matching print 4½" squares from a fat eighth and pair them up with the five 4½" squares that match the triangles from step 2. Lay out the nine squares as shown and sew them together in rows. Sew the rows together to make the nine-patch unit.

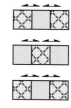

4 Match the center of a triangle from step 2 with the center of the nine-patch unit, and pin in place with wrong sides together and raw edges aligned. Sew the units together and press. Repeat for all four sides. This will complete your block, which should measure 17½" x 17½".

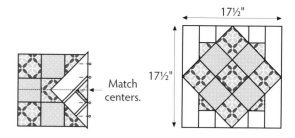

Match centers.

17½"

17½"

5 Repeat steps 1–4 to make a total of 12 blocks.

Aligning Seams

You can always press a seam open lightly with your fingernail to check the placement before setting the seam with your iron. If your placement is off, simply use your seam ripper to pull out your stitches and try again.

ASSEMBLING THE QUILT TOP

1 Arrange your blocks into four rows of three blocks each in an order that is pleasing to your eye. Once you're happy with the layout, sew the blocks in each row together, pressing seam allowances open as you go. Refer to the quilt assembly diagram on page 43.

2 Sew the rows together in pairs, and then sew the two pairs together. Press the seam allowances open.

3 The addition of the white border gives the illusion that the blocks are partially "floating." Sew the white 2½" x 51½" strips to the top and bottom of the quilt center. Press the seam allowances open. Sew the white 2½" x 72½" strips to the sides. Press.

FINISHING THE QUILT

1 Piece the backing together using a horizontal seam. The backing should measure at least 63" x 80".

2 Baste, quilt as desired, and bind. For more details, see "Finishing Your Quilts" on page 81.

see "Finishing Your Quilts" on page 81

Make It Your Own

One of the most exciting things about following a quilt pattern is putting your own twist on it. For this quilt, why not try using scraps for your nine patches? Or use one color for each block but vary the value of the color throughout the block? Above all, have fun with it!

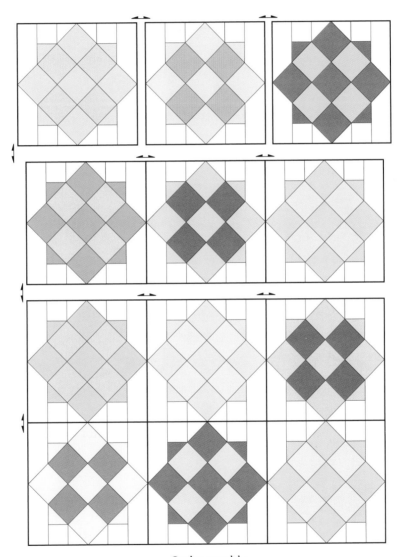

Quilt assembly

Finished quilt: 60" x 72" **Finished block:** 12" x 12"
Fabrics from various fabric collections

POLARIS

Stars have been a popular theme in quilting as far back as the early 1800s, recurring with countless variations and different twists on the classic shape. This quilt uses quarter-square-triangle units built from half-square-triangle units to create a scrappy variation of the traditional Ohio Star block. A quarter-square-triangle unit is just what it sounds like—a pieced square composed of four triangles, each of which is one-quarter of a square. These units may seem complicated, but they are really quite simple to put together, and this quilt will help you master the technique.

MATERIALS

Yardage is based on 42"-wide fabric.

3 yards of gray solid for block backgrounds

1 ⅛ yards total of assorted lime-green and yellow-green prints for blocks

1 ⅛ yards total of assorted maroon prints for blocks

⅞ yard total of assorted pink prints for blocks

⅞ yard total of assorted aqua and teal prints for blocks

⅝ yard of pink-striped fabric for binding

4 yards of fabric for backing

68" x 80" piece of batting

Make It Scrappy!

This is a great pattern for pulling together lots of different bits of fabric. Rather than using just one pink print or one blue print, use several—pick out some fat quarters or even fat eighths to give your quilt extra "pop."

If Bigger Is Better

Have your heart set on a queen-size quilt? You'll need to make 56 blocks, set 7 x 8, for an 84" x 96" finished size.

Materials

5¾ yards of fabric for block backgrounds

1⅞ yards total of assorted lime-green and yellow-green prints for blocks

1⅞ yards total of assorted maroon prints for blocks

1⅓ yards total of assorted pink prints for blocks

1⅓ yards total of assorted aqua and teal prints for blocks

⅞ yard of fabric for binding

8 yards of fabric for backing

92" x 104" piece of batting

CUTTING

From the pink prints, cut:
   22 squares, 6" x 6"

From the aqua and teal prints, cut:
   22 squares, 6" x 6"

From the green prints, cut:
   23 squares, 6" x 6"
   15 squares, 4½" x 4½"

From the maroon prints, cut:
   23 squares, 6" x 6"
   15 squares, 4½" x 4½"

Continued on page 46

From the gray solid, cut:
15 strips, 4½" x 42"; crosscut into 120 squares, 4½" x 4½"
5 strips, 6" x 42"; crosscut into 30 squares, 6" x 6"

From the binding fabric, cut:
7 strips, 2½" x 42"

PIECING THE BLOCKS

Use a scant ¼" seam allowance and press seam allowances open after sewing each seam.

1 On the wrong side of each gray 6" square, draw a diagonal line from corner to corner using a fabric marker or pencil and a ruler. Layer each marked square right sides together with a print 6" square. (You'll only use about a third of your 6" print squares in this step. Be sure to use a variety of prints, rather than just one.) Sew a scant ¼" from the drawn line on both sides. Do not sew on the line itself.

2 On your cutting mat, align your ruler with the drawn line and cut along it with a rotary cutter. Press seam allowances open. You will have 60 units.

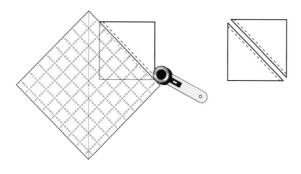

Make 60.

3 Place a unit from step 2 on your cutting mat and trim to 4½" square, aligning the 45° line of the ruler with the seam. After trimming, cut

the trimmed unit in half diagonally from corner to corner. Repeat to make 120 triangle units.

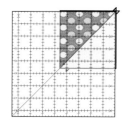

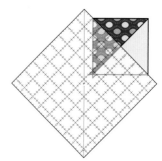

Make 120.

4 Repeat steps 1–3, replacing the gray square with a print square. Make triangle units with all of the remaining print 6" squares.

5 Choose one print triangle unit from step 4 and one gray/print triangle unit from step 3. Place them right sides together and pin at the seam. Sew the units together and press. Repeat to make 120 quarter-square-triangle units.

Make 120.

6 Arrange four of the units from step 5, four gray 4½" squares, and one maroon or green 4½" square as shown. Sew the units and squares together in rows and press. Sew the rows together to complete the block. Make a total of 30. Each block should measure 12½" x 12½".

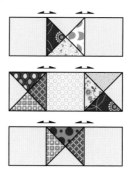 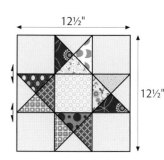

Make 30.

ASSEMBLING THE QUILT TOP

1 Arrange your blocks into six rows of five blocks each in an order that is pleasing to your eye. Once you're happy with the layout, sew the blocks together into rows, pressing the seam allowances open as you go.

2 Sew the rows together. Press.

FINISHING THE QUILT

1 Piece the backing together using a horizontal seam. The backing should measure at least 68" x 80".

2 Baste, quilt as desired, and bind. For more details, see "Finishing Your Quilts" on page 81.

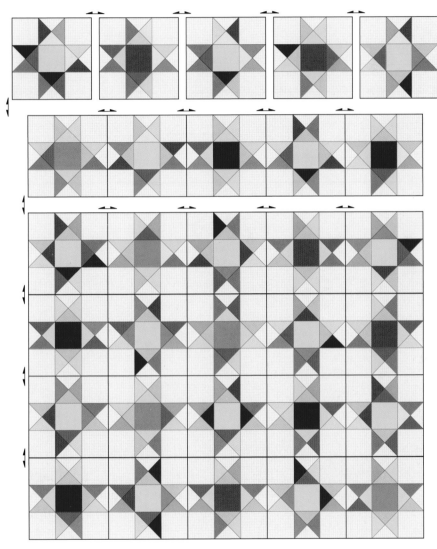

Quilt assembly

Finished quilt: 70" x 75"   **Finished block:** 12" x 6"
Fabrics from various Dear Stella Fabrics collections

DIAMONDS ARE A GIRL'S BEST FRIEND

*D*iamonds are one of my favorite geometric shapes, but rotary cutting them for a quilt can be a time-consuming task. In this project, you'll create diamond shapes by using two triangles that you can cut either with templates or with a pair of specialty rulers. Templates and specialty rulers can be a great help for cutting tricky shapes accurately with a rotary cutter. My favorite part about this quilt is the way the diamonds appear to float on the background, thanks to the skinny sashing around each diamond block.

MATERIALS

Yardage is based on 42"-wide fabric.

3½ yards of light-gray solid for block back-grounds and sashing

1⅓ yards total of assorted blue prints for blocks

⅔ yard total of assorted gray prints for blocks

⅝ yard of dark-gray solid for border

¼ yard of yellow print for blocks

⅔ yard of dark-blue print for binding

4¾ yards of fabric for backing

78" x 83" piece of batting

Tri-Recs Tools, freezer paper, or template plastic

Recommended Rulers

When cutting the pieces for this quilt, I highly recommend the Tri-Recs Tools set (designed by Darlene Zimmerman and Joy Hoffman for EZ Quilting). One triangle (tri) paired with two half-rectangles (recs) cre-ates the half-diamond unit that makes up this quilt block.

CUTTING

From the gray prints, cut:
3 strips, 6½" x 42"

From the blue prints, cut:
6 strips, 6½" x 42"

From the yellow print, cut:
1 strip, 6½" x 42"

From the light-gray solid, cut:
10 strips, 6½" x 42"
29 strips, 1½" x 42"; cut 7 strips into 40 rect-angles, 1½" x 6½"

From the dark-gray solid, cut:
8 strips, 2½" x 42"

From the binding fabric, cut:
8 strips, 2½" x 42"

CUTTING THE DIAMONDS

1 If you aren't using the Tri-Recs rulers, make templates A and B from freezer paper, template plastic, or even copy paper using the patterns on page 52. I find that the easiest way to make a template is to photocopy the pattern, cut it out, and use the paper copy in conjunction with a clear quilting ruler to cut out the pieces. If you prefer to work with something sturdier, you can glue your paper template to cardboard from a cereal box and then cut it out.

2 Fold a print 6½" x 42" strip in half on your cutting mat, lining up the raw edges and selvage edges. Trim off the selvage edges. Using either the tri ruler or template A, lay the top edge of the ruler or template along the top of the strip. Cut along both sides of the ruler/template. If you're using the paper template, place a clear acrylic ruler on top, aligning the edge with the edge of the template. Then cut along the side of the ruler, being careful not to trim the edges of the paper. Reposition the ruler to cut the second side.

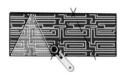 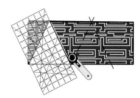

3 Rotate the ruler/template so that the tip is pointing downward and is aligned with the bottom edge of the strip and the newly cut edge. Cut a second triangle. Continue rotating and cutting to create a total of 100 print triangles in 50 matching pairs. You should be able to cut 10 triangles (5 pairs) per strip.

 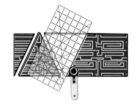

Cut 50 matching pairs.

4 Fold a light-gray 6½" x 42" strip in half on your cutting mat, lining up the raw edges and selvage edges. Trim off the selvage edges. Using either the rec ruler or template B, cut triangles in the same manner as before. Rotate and cut a total of 200 triangles. You should be able to cut 20 triangles per strip.

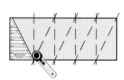 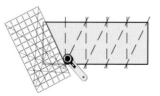

Cut 200 triangles.

PIECING THE BLOCKS

Use a scant ¼" seam allowance and press seam allowances open or as directed after sewing each seam.

1 With right sides together, lay a gray triangle on one side of a print triangle, aligning the raw edges and squared-off ends. Stitch the pieces together and press the seam allowances away from the print triangle. Sew a second gray triangle to the opposite side and press. Repeat with a matching print triangle to make two identical units.

Make 2.

2 Place the two units right sides together and align the edges. Pin at the seams and sew the units together as shown. Press the seam allowances open. The block should measure 12½" x 6½".

 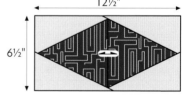

3 Repeat steps 1 and 2 to make a total of 50 blocks.

ASSEMBLING THE QUILT TOP

1 Arrange your blocks into 10 rows of five blocks each in an order that is pleasing to your eye. Once you're happy with the layout, add the light-gray 1½" x 6½" sashing rectangles between the blocks in each row. Sew the pieces together into rows, pressing the seam allowances open as you go.

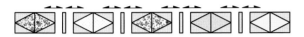

2 Sew the light-gray 1½" x 42" strips together end to end to make one long strip. Press the seam allowances open. From the long strip, cut 11 strips, 1½" x 64½", and two strips, 1½" x 71½".

3 Sew the rows together with the 64½"-long sashing strips. Press seam allowances open. Add the 71½"-long strips to the sides. Press.

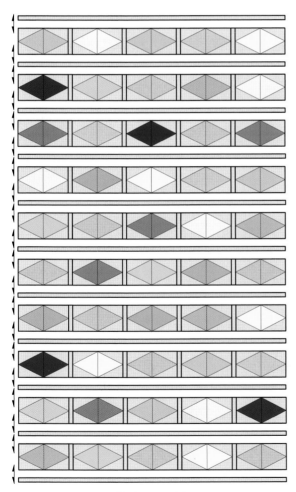

Quilt assembly

4 Sew the dark-gray 2½" x 42" strips together in pairs to make four long strips. Cut two strips, 2½" x 66½", and sew them to the top and bottom of the quilt center. Cut two strips, 2½" x 75½", and sew them to the sides. Press.

FINISHING THE QUILT

1 Piece the backing together using a vertical seam. The backing should measure at least 78" x 83".

2 Baste, quilt as desired, and bind. For more details, see "Finishing Your Quilts" on page 81.

Get Moody

Playing with fabrics and colors can completely change the mood of a quilt. For this mini version of "Diamonds Are a Girl's Best Friend," I made four diamond blocks using fun prints from Sweetwater's Lucy's Crab Shack collection for Moda Fabrics. A white tone-on-tone print provides a neutral backdrop. These completely different fabric choices take this quilt from a sophisticated, grown-up feel to a more fun, playful vibe.

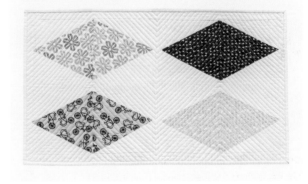

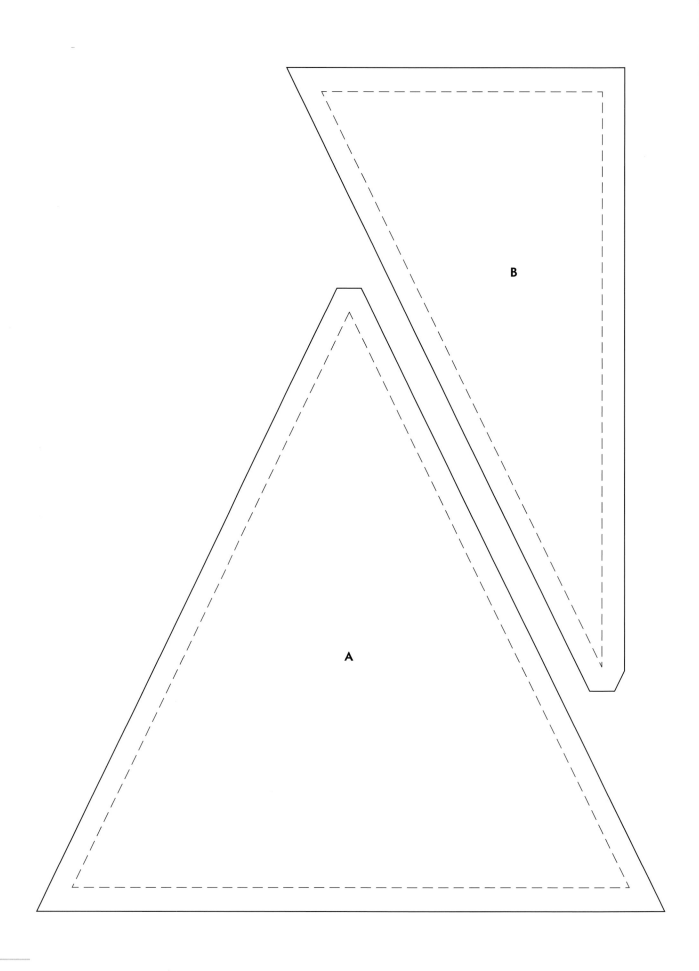

B

A

X MARKS THE SPOT

Patchwork can be a fabulous exercise in controlled creativity, but sometimes it's a lot of fun to give up control and let random selection rule the day. With this quilt top, I placed my blocks haphazardly throughout the layout, blindly grabbing blocks and putting them together rather than positioning each one carefully, as I normally would. The randomness of it all left me with a wonderfully free feeling. Not up for going random? You could create a stunning flow throughout this quilt by staggering your blocks by color.

MATERIALS

Yardage is based on 42"-wide fabric.

15 fat quarters of assorted prints for blocks

2 yards of white solid for blocks

⅝ yard of navy solid for binding

3½ yards of fabric for backing

61" x 71" piece of batting

CUTTING

From each of the 15 fat quarters, cut:
  2 squares, 3" x 3"
  8 rectangles, 3" x 5½"
  4 squares, 2¾" x 2¾"; cut in half diagonally to yield 8 triangles

From the white solid, cut:
  30 squares, 8⅜" x 8⅜"; cut into quarters diagonally to yield 120 triangles

From the binding fabric, cut:
  6 strips, 2½" x 42"

PIECING THE BLOCKS

Use a scant ¼" seam allowance and press seam allowances open after sewing each seam.

1 Pair a print triangle with a matching 3" x 5½" rectangle. With right sides together, align the long edge of the triangle with a short end of the rectangle, centering the rectangle on the triangle. Sew the pieces together and press. Make four matching units.

Make 4.

2 Sew a white triangle to one side of a unit from step 1, aligning the short edge of the triangle with the long edge of the rectangle. Press and repeat for the opposite side of the unit. Make two.

Make 2.

Finished quilt: 52½" x 63" **Finished block:** 10½" x 10½"

Fabrics from Lotta Jansdotter's Echo collection for Windham Fabrics

3 Sew the remaining two units from step 1 to opposite sides of a contrasting print 3" square as shown to make the block center.

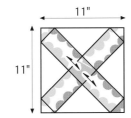

4 Sew a unit from step 2 to each side of the center unit. Press carefully and measure your block. It should measure 11" x 11". Trim as needed to square up the block.

5 Repeat steps 1–4 to make a total of 30 blocks.

ASSEMBLING THE QUILT TOP

1 Arrange your blocks into six rows of five blocks each in an order that is pleasing to your eye. Once you're happy with the layout, sew the blocks in each row together. Press the seam allowances open as you go.

2 Sew the rows together in pairs, and then sew the pairs together. Press.

FINISHING THE QUILT

1 Piece the backing together using a horizontal seam. The backing should measure at least 61" x 71".

2 Baste, quilt as desired, and bind. For more details, see "Finishing Your Quilts" on page 81.

Quilt assembly

Finished quilt: 66½" x 87½" **Finished block:** 14" x 12"

Fabrics from my scrap bins

RAINBOW CAKES

As you make more and more quilts, you will accumulate lots of scraps. Some quilters have the most fun working with their scraps and turning those little pieces into something wonderful. This bright, fun project is a great way to dig through your own scraps and put together a scrapbook quilt with assorted bits from the other quilts you've made. If you don't have enough scraps for the whole thing, no worries—fabric companies offer plenty of small precut pieces such as fat quarters, fat eighths, 2½"-wide strips, and 10" squares, all just waiting to come to your rescue!

MATERIALS

Yardage is based on 42"-wide fabric.

2⅞ yards of light-gray solid for blocks and sashing

⅝ yard each of assorted pink, red, orange, yellow, green, blue, and purple scraps (4⅜ yards total)

⅔ yard of black-and-white print for binding

5⅓ yards of fabric for backing

75" x 96" piece of batting

CUTTING

In the quilt shown, I worked with scraps and cut rectangles of varying widths for each "layer" of the cake blocks. For the sake of simplicity, however, these cutting instructions will result in uniformly sized rectangles. Feel free to be as creative with sizes as you like; just make sure that the bottom layer measures 6½" x 14½", the middle layer measures 4½" x 10½", and the top layer measures 2½" x 6½".

From each of the assorted pink, red, orange, yellow, green, blue, and purple scraps, cut:
24 rectangles, 2½" x 6½"
24 rectangles, 2" x 4½"
24 rectangles, 1⅜" x 2½"

From the light-gray solid, cut:
12 strips, 2½" x 42"; crosscut into 96 rectangles, 2½" x 4½"
15 strips, 3" x 42"; crosscut 6 strips into 18 strips, 3" x 12½"
8 strips, 2" x 42"

From the binding fabric, cut:
8 strips, 2½" x 42"

If Bigger Is Better

If your scrap box is overflowing, then a king-size quilt could be the solution! You'll need to make 48 blocks, set 6 x 8, for a 99½" x 116½" finished size.

Materials

5⅝ yards of light-gray solid for blocks and sashing

1¼ yards total of assorted pink scraps for blocks

1¼ yards total of assorted red scraps for blocks

1¼ yards total of assorted orange scraps for blocks

1¼ yards total of assorted yellow scraps for blocks

1¼ yards total of assorted green scraps for blocks

1¼ yards total of assorted blue scraps for blocks

1¼ yards total of assorted purple scraps for blocks

1 yard of black-and-white print for binding

9¼ yards of fabric for backing

108" x 124" piece of batting

PIECING THE BLOCKS

Use a scant ¼" seam allowance and press seam allowances open after sewing each seam.

1 For the bottom layer of the cake block, sew one 2½" x 6½" rectangle of each color together in rainbow order: pink, red, orange, yellow, green, blue, and purple. Measure, and trim to 6½" x 14½" if necessary.

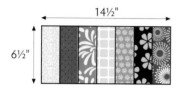

2 For the middle layer, sew one 2" x 4½" rectangle of each color together in the same order: pink, red, orange, yellow, green, blue, and purple. Trim to 4½" x 10½". Sew a gray 2½" x 4½" rectangle to each end of the unit as shown.

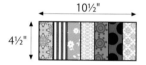

3 For the top layer, sew one 1⅜" x 2½" rectangle of each color together in the same order: pink, red, orange, yellow, green, blue, and purple. Trim to 2½" x 6½". Sew a gray 2½" x 4½" rectangle to each end of the unit as shown.

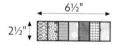

4 Sew the bottom and middle layers together. Then add the top layer, aligning the raw edges, and press.

Make 24.

5 Repeat steps 1–4 to make a total of 24 blocks.

ASSEMBLING THE QUILT TOP

1 Arrange your blocks into six rows of four blocks each in an order that is pleasing to your eye. Rotating every other block adds a sense of movement to the quilt. Once you're happy with the layout, add the gray 3" x 12½" sashing pieces between the blocks in each row. Sew the pieces together into rows, pressing seam allowances open as you go.

2 Sew the remaining gray 3" x 42" strips together end to end to make one long strip. Cut into five sashing strips 64" long.

3 Sew the rows together with the sashing strips, first sewing them in pairs and then sewing the pairs together. Press.

4 Sew the gray 2" x 42" strips together to make one long strip. Cut two strips, 2" x 85". Sew these to the sides of the quilt top. Press. Cut two strips, 2" x 66 1/2", and sew these to the top and bottom of the quilt top. Press.

FINISHING THE QUILT

1 Piece the backing together using a vertical seam. The backing should measure at least 75" x 96".

2 Baste, quilt as desired, and bind. For more details, see "Finishing Your Quilts" on page 81.

Managing Your Scraps

Creating scraps is one of the side effects of making quilts, and once you begin to build up lots of scraps, you'll be able to make quilts strictly from those wonderful little bits of fabric. I love creating scrap quilts—the scraps always remind me of past projects I've made for friends and family. I sort my scraps in two ways: by size and by color. I have one bin of scraps that are skinny, between 1" and 2½" wide, and I use those pieces in string quilts and string projects. My other scrap bins are strictly sorted by color, and I use those scraps in quilts as well as pillows and other small projects.

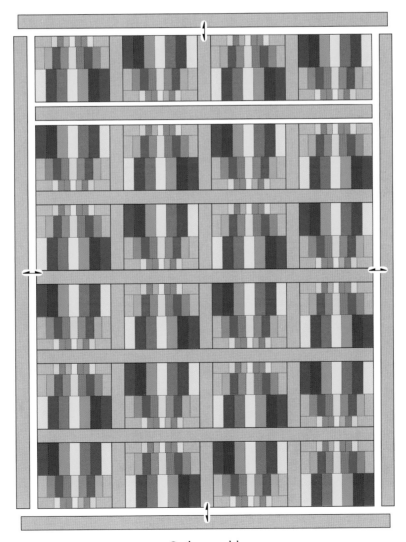

Quilt assembly

Finished quilt: 48" x 60"   **Finished block:** 12" x 12"
Fabrics from Parson Gray's Curious Nature collection for Free Spirit Fabrics

LATTICE OF STARS

*T*he Lattice of Stars block begins with a simple sawtooth star—a classic, traditional block design—and frames it within a diamond, creating the illusion that the block is set on point. I especially love the way the frame creates a lattice effect across the quilt top. When selecting fabrics, keep in mind that you need several different values within each block for contrast. In this quilt, you'll work with both half-square-triangle units and flying-geese units, which are valuable building blocks for a well-rounded patchwork repertoire.

MATERIALS

Yardage is based on 42"-wide fabric.

1⅞ yards total of assorted prints for star backgrounds

1¾ yards of taupe solid for blocks*

1⅛ yards total of assorted prints for block corners

⅞ yard total of assorted prints for star points

½ yard total of assorted prints for star centers

½ yard of dark print for binding

3¼ yards of fabric for backing

56" x 68" piece of batting

This fabric will create the diamond "lattice."

CUTTING

From the assorted prints for star centers, cut:
   20 squares, 4½" x 4½"

From the assorted prints for star points, cut:
   20 sets of 8 squares, 2½" x 2½" (160 total)

From the assorted prints for star backgrounds, cut:
   20 sets of 8 rectangles, 2½" x 4½" (160 total)
   2 squares, 3¼" x 3¼" (40 total)

From the assorted prints for block corners, cut:
   20 sets of 4 squares, 2½" x 2½" (80 total)
   4 squares, 3¼" x 3¼" (80 total)

From the taupe solid, cut:
   10 strips, 3¼" x 42"; crosscut into 120 squares, 3¼" x 3¼"
   10 strips, 2½" x 42"; crosscut into 160 squares, 2½" x 2½"

From the binding fabric, cut:
   6 strips, 2½" x 42"

PIECING THE BLOCKS

Use a scant ¼" seam allowance and press seam allowances open after sewing each seam unless directed otherwise. For each block, you'll make eight flying-geese units and eight half-square-triangle units, so you'll get plenty of practice with these useful techniques.

1 To make the star points, also known as flying-geese units, draw a diagonal line from corner to corner on the wrong side of two 2½" squares of star-point fabric using a ruler and fabric marker. Place a marked square on one end of a 2½" x 4½" background rectangle as shown, right sides together. Sew on the drawn line. Trim excess fabric, leaving a ¼" seam allowance beyond the stitching. Press the seam allowances toward the star-point fabric, rather than open. Sew the second marked square to the opposite end of the rectangle, trim, and press. Make four matching flying-geese units.

Make 4.

2 Repeat step 1 using taupe 2½" squares and 2½" x 4½" rectangles of the same background print. Make four matching flying-geese units.

Make 4.

3 Draw a diagonal line from corner to corner on the wrong side of six taupe 3¼" squares.

4 Pair a marked taupe square with a 3¼" square of the same background print, right sides together. Sew ¼" from the drawn line on each side. Using a ruler and rotary cutter, cut along the diagonal line. Press the seam allowances open. Repeat with another pair of squares to make a total of four half-square-triangle units. Press seam allowances open.

Make 4.

5 Using a square ruler and rotary cutter, trim each half-square-triangle unit to 2½" x 2½". See "Trimming Half-Square-Triangle Units" at right for details.

6 Repeat steps 4 and 5 with the remaining marked taupe squares and four matching 3¼" squares for block corners. Make eight half-square-triangle units.

Make 8.

Trimming Half-Square-Triangle Units

You may have noticed the diagonal lines on your quilting rulers. Most quilting rulers are printed with two such lines, representing a 45° angle and a 60° angle. To trim half-square-triangle units, simply align the 45° line with the seam along the diagonal of your sewn unit and trim as necessary. Sometimes you'll only need to trim one or two sides of the unit; sometimes you'll need to trim all four. It just depends on your accuracy and whether the pieces were cut oversize. The cutting instructions for this quilt include oversize squares; you'll probably need to trim all four sides. Do this by cutting the right and top edges of the unit first. Then rotate the unit 180° and trim the remaining two edges.

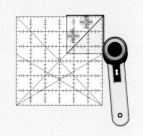 

7 Arrange the half-square-triangle units, the flying-geese units, the matching 2½" squares for block corners, and a 4½" center square as shown. Sew the units into rows and press. Sew the rows together, pinning at each seam to ensure everything lines up just right.

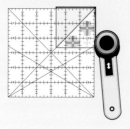  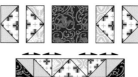 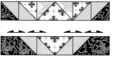

8 Repeat steps 1–7 to make a total of 20 blocks.

ASSEMBLING THE QUILT TOP

1 Arrange your blocks into five rows of four blocks each in an order that is pleasing to your eye. Once you're happy with the layout, sew the blocks in each row together, pressing seam allowances open as you go.

2 Sew the rows together in pairs, and then sew the pairs together. Press.

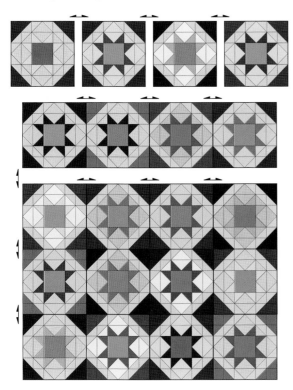

Quilt assembly

FINISHING THE QUILT

1 Piece the backing together using a horizontal seam. The backing should measure at least 56" x 68".

2 Baste, quilt as desired, and bind. For more details, see "Finishing Your Quilts" on page 81.

Just for Fun

Using one Lattice of Stars block, I created an adorable mini-quilt, perfect to hang in my sewing room. This little cutie uses fabrics from Violet Craft's amazing Madrona Road collection for Michael Miller Fabrics. I also used a cathedral windows style of free-motion quilting, connecting the arcs to create a look very similar to a traditional Cathedral Windows quilt block.

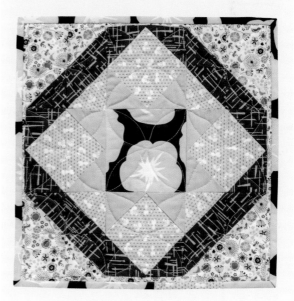

Finished quilt: 65" x 90" **Finished block:** 10" x 18"
Fabrics from various collections paired with Art Gallery solids

*T*he rectangular blocks in this quilt create stacks of beads that remind me of the friendship bracelets I used to make as a kid. I remember how much I prized my large collection of embroidery floss, much like the way I prize my fabric stash these days. One of my favorite things about this design is the creation of negative space that reigns throughout the quilt surface—a great example of how "empty" spaces between blocks can influence the look of your quilt as much as the blocks themselves. The use of negative space is one of the hallmarks of the modern quilting movement.

MATERIALS

Yardage is based on 42"-wide fabric. Note that aqua refers to the light blue-green colors and teal refers to the dark blue-green colors.

4 yards of white solid for blocks and background

½ yard of aqua solid for blocks and vertical strips

½ yard of gold solid for blocks and vertical strips

⅓ yard of teal solid for blocks and vertical strips

1 fat eighth *each* of 7 assorted teal prints for blocks

1 fat eighth *each* of 5 assorted aqua prints for blocks

1 fat eighth *each* of 3 assorted gold prints for blocks

⅔ yard of gold print for binding

5½ yards of fabric for backing

73" x 98" piece of batting

CUTTING

From the aqua solid, cut:
7 strips, 2½" x 18½"
2 strips, 2½" x 42"

From *each* of the 5 aqua prints, cut:
6 squares, 3¼" x 3¼"
2 rectangles, 2½" x 6½"

From the teal solid, cut:
3 strips, 2½" x 18½"
1 strip, 2½" x 36½"

From *each* of the 7 teal prints, cut:
6 squares, 3¼" x 3¼"
2 rectangles, 2½" x 6½"

From the gold solid, cut:
6 strips, 2½" x 18½"
2 strips, 2½" x 42"

From *each* of the 3 gold prints, cut:
6 squares, 3¼" x 3¼"
2 rectangles, 2½" x 6½"

From the white solid, cut:
10 strips, 4½" x 42"; cut 3 *strips* into:
    2 strips, 4½" x 36½"
    2 strips, 4½" x 18½"
14 strips, 3" x 42"
8 strips, 3¼" x 42"; crosscut into 90 squares, 3¼" x 3¼"
17 strips, 2½" x 42"; crosscut into:
    60 squares, 2½" x 2½"
    30 rectangles, 2½" x 6½"
    60 rectangles, 2½" x 4½"

From the binding fabric, cut:
8 strips, 2½" x 42"

PIECING THE BLOCKS

Use a scant ¼" seam allowance and press seam allowances open after sewing each seam.

1 Draw a diagonal line from corner to corner on the wrong side of each white 3¼" square.

2 Pair a marked white square with an aqua-print 3¼" square, right sides together and raw edges aligned. Sew a scant ¼" from the drawn line on each side. Cut on the line. Press and trim the half-square-triangle units to 2½" x 2½". Refer to "Trimming Half-Square-Triangle Units" on page 62 for details. Make a total of 12 matching units.

Make 12.

3 Using the same aqua print, sew an aqua 2½" x 6½" rectangle to a white 2½" x 6½" rectangle as shown. Make two.

Make 2.

4 Arrange one white 2½" square and three half-square-triangle units together as shown. Sew the squares into rows and then sew the rows together. Make four.

Make 4.

5 Arrange the units from steps 3 and 4 with two white 2½" x 4½" rectangles as shown. Sew the units together. Make two block sections.

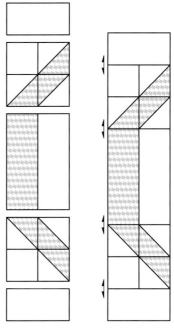

Make 2.

6 Sew a gold solid 2½" x 18½" strip between the two sections from step 5. The block should measure 10½" x 18½".

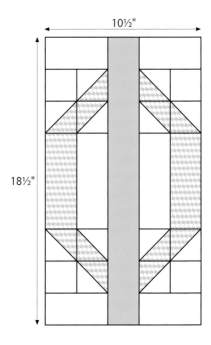

7 Repeat steps 1–6 to make a total of 15 Bead blocks: four aqua blocks with gold centers, six teal blocks with aqua centers, one teal block with a gold center, one aqua block with an aqua center, and three gold blocks with teal centers.

ASSEMBLING THE QUILT TOP

The quilt is assembled in columns of Bead blocks and pieced sections. The pieced sections consist of three strips of fabric—one of the solids flanked by two white 4½"-wide strips. Refer to the quilt assembly diagram on page 68 as you sew the columns together. When joining long strips, take care to keep the raw edges aligned for the length of the strips, as they have a tendency to shift during sewing.

1 Sew the two gold 2½" x 42" strips together to make one long strip. Cut one strip, 2½" x 72½".

2 Sew four white 4½" x 42" strips together to make one long strip. Cut two strips, 4½" x 72½".

3 Sew the white strips from step 2 to the sides of the gold strip from step 1. Sew this pieced section to an aqua Bead block with gold center to make column 1.

4 Sew the two aqua 2½" x 42" strips together to make one long strip. Cut one strip, 2½" x 54½".

5 Sew three white 4½" x 42" strips together to make one long strip. Cut two strips, 4½" x 54½".

6 Sew the white strips from step 5 to the sides of the aqua strip from step 4. Sew this pieced section together with two teal Bead blocks with aqua centers to make column 2.

7 Sew the two white 4½" x 36½" strips to the sides of the teal 2½" x 36½" strip. Sew this pieced section together with three gold Bead blocks with teal centers to make column 3.

8 Sew the two white 4½" x 18½" strips to the sides of the remaining gold 2½" x 18½" strip. Sew this pieced section together with one teal and three aqua Bead blocks with gold centers to make column 4.

Quick-and-Easy Option

Here's another way to make half-square-triangle units. Once you've tried the method described in steps 1 and 2 of "Piecing The Blocks," you might want to experiment with this quick and easy alternative. With this method, you'll make four identical half-square-triangle units from a pair of squares cut oversize.

1 To make four finished units that measure 2" x 2", cut one light square and one medium or dark square, 4½" x 4½". (Add 2½" to the desired finished size.)

2 Layer the two squares right sides together and sew ¼" from the edges all around the squares.

3 Using a ruler and rotary cutter, cut the square into quarters diagonally. Press the seam allowances open and trim, following the instructions in "Trimming Half-Square-Triangle Units" on page 62. Be sure to trim ½" larger than the desired finished size, and be very careful when handling and sewing the trimmed units, as they will have bias edges. You'll have four identical units.

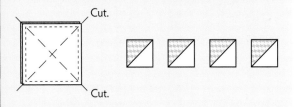

Size Your Squares

To repeat this method on your own, simply add 2½" to the desired finished size of the half-square-triangle units. This not only gives you enough fabric to make your half-square-triangle units, but also makes your units slightly oversized to allow for trimming.

9 Sew the remaining five Bead blocks with aqua centers together to make column 5.

10 Sew the white 3" x 42" strips together to make one long strip. Cut six sashing strips, 3" x 90½". Sew the sashing and columns together to complete the quilt top. Press.

FINISHING THE QUILT

1 Piece the backing together using a vertical seam. The backing should measure at least 73" x 98".

2 Baste, quilt as desired, and bind. For more details, see "Finishing Your Quilts" on page 81.

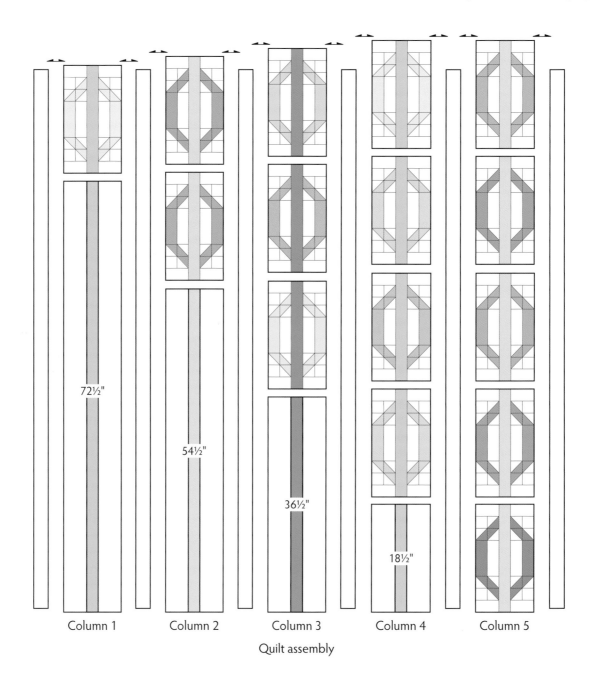

72½"

54½"

36½"

18½"

Column 1   Column 2   Column 3   Column 4   Column 5

Quilt assembly

WONKY FENCES

*I*mprovisational piecing is quite popular within the modern quilting movement, but many quilters are hesitant to give it a try. This quilt pattern, a skewed variation of the traditional Rail Fence block, gives you the chance to enjoy wonky piecing in a somewhat planned, calculated way. This is also a great project for getting your feet wet with angled seams. After this quilt, you'll be ready to throw yourself into a completely improvised design, with lots of random piecing.

MATERIALS

Yardage is based on 42"-wide fabric.

16 fat quarters of assorted prints for blocks

½ yard of print for binding

3¼ yards of fabric for backing

58" x 68" piece of batting

If Bigger Is Better

So you want to make a queen-size quilt? You'll need to make 90 blocks, set 9 x 10, for a 90" x 100" finished size.

Materials

46 fat quarters of assorted prints for blocks

⅞ yard of fabric for binding

8¼ yards of fabric for backing

98" x 108" piece of batting

CUTTING

From *each* of the 16 fat quarters, cut:
  2 rectangles, 10½" x 13"

From the binding fabric, cut:
  6 strips, 2½" x 42"

PIECING THE BLOCKS

Use a scant ¼" seam allowance and press seam allowances open after sewing each seam.

1 Choose four different 10½" x 13" rectangles. This group of fabrics will make four blocks, so be sure your rectangles have variety and work well together. Stack the rectangles right side up on your cutting mat, aligning the raw edges and lining up the stack with the grid lines on the mat.

2 Using the cutting mat's grid lines, place your ruler 3" from the bottom-right corner of the rectangle stack and 2" from the upper-right corner of the stack. Make your first cut along the right edge of the ruler. Do not move the fabric layers.

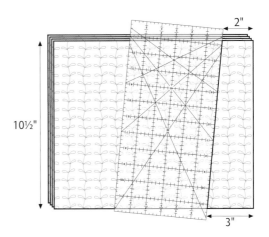

Finished quilt: 50" x 60"   **Finished block:** 10" x 10"

Fabrics from the Summerville collection by Lu Summers for Moda Fabrics

3 To make the second cut, place your ruler 6" from the bottom-right corner of the rectangle stack and 7½" from the upper-right corner. Cut along the right edge of the ruler, keeping the layers in position.

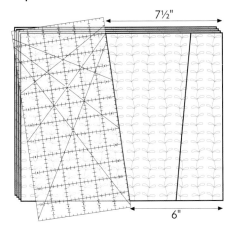

7½"

6"

4 For the third cut, place your ruler 12" from the bottom-right corner of the rectangle stack and 10" from the upper-right corner. Cut along the right edge of the ruler. You should have four wedge-shaped pieces.

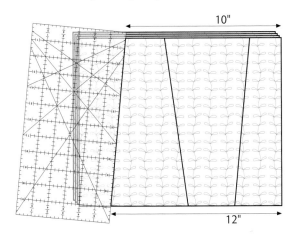

10"

12"

Make It Your Own

You can follow my instructions for making all of the blocks in a precise way, or you can get truly improvisational by making three random cuts along the short side of your stack of four rectangles. After cutting, piece as instructed to complete each group of four blocks. As long as you use a ruler to make your cuts, your pieces should line up and still create four 10½" squares. You might want to try one group of blocks using my measurements, and then vary the cutting for subsequent blocks.

5 Separate the first stack of wedges and make four separate piles. Separate the second stack of wedges and place one with each of the piles you just created, mixing up the fabrics. Repeat for the remaining two stacks and you should have four blocks, each with a different arrangement of fabrics.

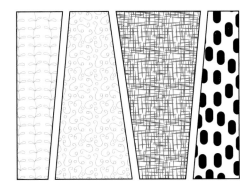

6 Sew the wedges together, offsetting the angled ends just slightly. Press all seam allowances open.

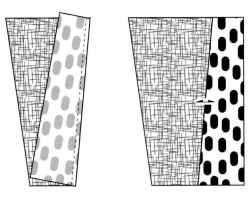

7 Place the pressed block on your cutting mat and trim to 10½" x 10½".

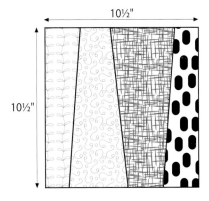

10½"

10½"

8 Repeat steps 1–7 to make a total of 30 blocks. You'll have enough pieces for 32 blocks if you want to have extras to choose from.

ASSEMBLING THE QUILT TOP

1 Arrange your blocks into six rows of five blocks each in an order that is pleasing to your eye. Rotate every other block to create more movement and visual interest. Once you're happy with the layout, sew the blocks in each row together, pressing the seam allowances open as you go.

2 Sew the rows together. Press.

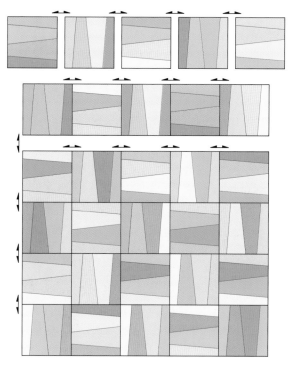

Quilt assembly

FINISHING THE QUILT

1 Piece the backing together using a horizontal seam. The backing should measure at least 58" x 68".

2 Baste, quilt as desired, and bind. For more details, see "Finishing Your Quilts" on page 81.

Working with Solids

Improvisational quilts made with solid fabrics are some of my personal favorites. For a different look, I used four gorgeous Michael Miller Cotton Couture solids in bright, vivid colors. I quilted this smaller version of "Wonky Fences" using random straight-line quilting, which is a great way to complement an improvisational quilt.

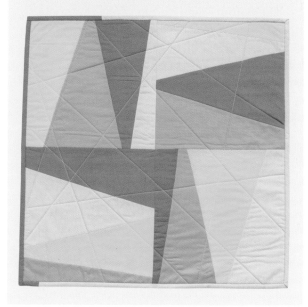

WHAM

Foundation piecing yields incredibly accurate results, allowing you to create shapes and angles that are tricky to accomplish with regular piecing. When you foundation piece on paper, you sew your fabric onto a paper pattern printed with seam lines. The fabric is pinned to the plain side of the paper, and you stitch directly along the printed lines. The technique can also be executed with fabric rather than paper as the foundation, but that can create heavier quilt blocks, as the extra layer of fabric stays within the quilt. Paper foundations have the advantage of being easy to remove after your blocks are complete.

MATERIALS

Yardage is based on 42"-wide fabric.

4½ yards total of assorted prints for blocks

4½ yards total of assorted coordinating solids for blocks

1 yard of green print for outer border

½ yard of chocolate-brown solid for inner border

⅝ yard of print for binding or scraps

3⅓ yards of fabric for backing

60" x 73" piece of batting

Foundation-piecing paper or copy paper

Scrappy Bindings

A great way to add a pop of color to your finished quilts is to create a scrappy binding using your scraps. You could also choose a binding fabric and add just one or two scraps pieced into the binding.

CUTTING

The cutting dimensions for blocks are a bit larger than necessary, designed to allow more than enough fabric to cover each part of the paper pattern as well as the seam allowances. Paper foundation piecing is a great way to use irregular scraps of fabric, and your cutting doesn't need to be quite as precise as usual, since the fabric is cut oversize.

Cutting for 1 Block (Cut 24 total.)

From 1 of the assorted prints, cut:
   4 squares, 5" x 5"
   4 rectangles, 3" x 5"
   4 squares, 3" x 3"

From 1 of the assorted solids, cut:
   4 squares, 5" x 5"
   4 rectangles, 3" x 5"
   4 squares, 3" x 3"

Cutting for Borders and Binding

From the chocolate-brown solid, cut:
   5 strips, 3" x 42"

From the green print, cut:
   6 strips, 5" x 42"

From the binding fabric, cut:
   7 strips, 2½" x 42", or a total length of 250"

PIECING THE BLOCKS

Paper foundation piecing has grown in popularity among quilters over the years, and there are many different kinds of foundation paper on the market. I simply use printer paper from my office supplies, and it works quite well. Foundation papers are sold at quilt shops and craft stores, and those papers are usually more transparent and can be removed quite easily. Experiment to find what works best for you.

When sewing on paper foundations, I recommend using a shorter stitch length, between 1.25 mm and 1.5 mm (16 to 20 stitches per inch), to perforate the paper. This makes it easier to tear off the paper later without disturbing the stitching.

Finished quilt: 52¼" x 65" **Finished block:** 9" x 9"

Fabrics from Denyse Schmidt's Flea Market Fancy collection for Free Spirit Fabrics,
paired with various Free Spirit Designer Solids

Don't go any shorter with your stitch length, though, or your paper may become perforated to the point that it starts to fall apart as you're stitching.

1 Using the foundation patterns on page 79 and a photocopy machine, make 96 copies of pattern A and 96 copies of pattern B. Be sure to copy the patterns at 100%. Cut out each pattern piece, leaving some space beyond the seam allowance.

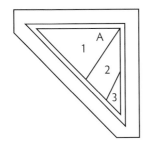

2 Each section of the paper pattern is numbered to show the piecing sequence. Starting with pattern A, section 1, place a print 5" square wrong side down on the unprinted side of the foundation paper, making sure the fabric covers section 1 completely. It should extend beyond the triangle on all sides, and overlap the seam allowance between sections 1 and 2. To check your placement, hold the pattern up to a bright light source and look at the paper side. The fabric should overlap the line where sections 1 and 2 meet by at least ¼". Pin it in place through the foundation paper.

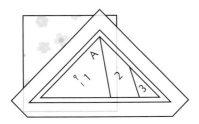

3 Choose a coordinating solid 3" x 5" rectangle, and place it right sides together with piece 1, aligning the raw edges along the line between sections 1 and 2. Pin in place, making sure to pin through the paper as well. You can check your placement by holding your finger where the seam will be and flipping piece 2 over to ensure that it covers section 2 on the paper, as well as the seam allowance at the top and bottom of piece 2. Again, use a light source if needed to make sure your fabric will cover the space for section 2.

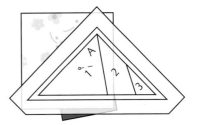

4 Shorten your stitch length (if you haven't already done so) and place your pinned paper pattern under the needle, paper side up. Stitch on the line between piece 1 and piece 2, backstitching at the start and end of the seam. You'll be putting pressure on these seams when you tear the paper off; backstitching will reinforce the seams.

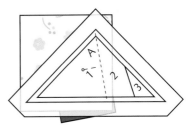

Mark Your Patterns

To keep my fabric plans straight when paper piecing, I often write or draw on my paper pieces, using highlighter or colored pencil to help myself remember which colored fabrics go where in the block.

5 Open up piece 2, making sure that it does indeed cover section 2 of the paper. Trim the excess fabric from the seam allowance, leaving ¼". I always trim with scissors, rather than a rotary cutter, since there's no need to measure and be precise here—you can just eyeball it and trim with scissors. Press piece 2 over the paper with a hot, dry iron. When working with a foundation, press seam allowances to one side. I typically finger-press the seam first, and then finish with the iron.

Trim.

6 Choose a print 3" x 3" square for piece 3 that matches the print you used for piece 1. Align the fabric right sides together with piece 2 and flip open to make sure it will cover all of section 3 on the paper pattern, as well as the seam allowance on the outside of the triangle.

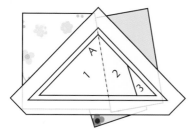

7 Pin in place through the paper and stitch on the line between piece 2 and piece 3, paper side up. Again, backstitch at the start and end of this seam. Open up piece 3, making sure that it covers the section 3 of the paper, and then trim the seam allowance to ¼". Press piece 3 over the section. Your pieced unit may look a little odd, but that's normal due to the oversize pieces.

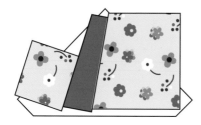

8 Press the entire unit with a hot, dry iron one more time and place it on your cutting mat for trimming. With a ruler and rotary cutter, trim along the outer solid black line all around the unit.

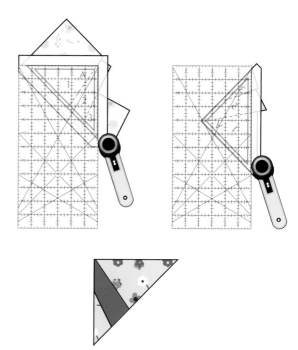

9 Remove the foundation paper by folding back the paper, starting with section 1; then crease along the seam and rip. Discard the paper and set aside your pieced unit. You can also wait until your block is complete to remove the paper. The paper helps to stabilize the edges of the units when sewing them together.

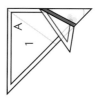 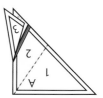

10 Repeat steps 2–9 to make two matching A units. Repeat steps 2–9 again, but swap the fabric placement: use the solid fabric for pieces 1 and 3 and the print fabric for piece 2. Make another set of two matching A units.

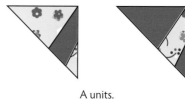

A units.
Make 2 of each.

11 Repeat steps 2–10 with pattern B to make two pairs of matching B units.

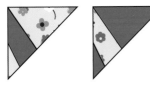

B units.
Make 2 of each.

12 Pair up the A and B units as shown, and sew them together along the short, pieced side of the triangles. Press the seam allowances open. Make two of each combination, for a total of four large triangles; each triangle is one-quarter of the block.

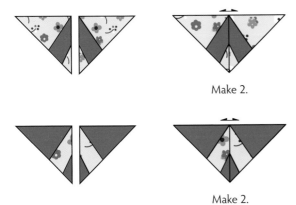

Make 2.

Make 2.

13 To complete the block, arrange the four triangles as shown. Sew the triangles together in pairs, and then sew the pairs together. Press seam allowances open. The block should measure 9½" x 9½".

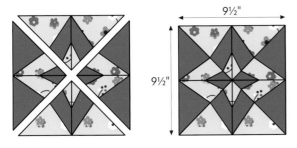

9½"

9½"

14 Repeat steps 2–13 to make a total of 18 blocks.

15 Repeat steps 2–12, sewing the triangles together in pairs to make 10 half blocks for the sides. Repeat steps 2–12 to make four quarter blocks for the corners.

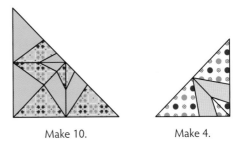

Make 10.   Make 4.

ASSEMBLING THE QUILT TOP

1 Arrange your blocks into diagonal rows as shown in the quilt assembly diagram below. Position the half blocks along the top, bottom, and sides, and add the quarter blocks in the corners. Sew the blocks in each row together, pressing seam allowances open as you go.

2 Sew the rows together. Press.

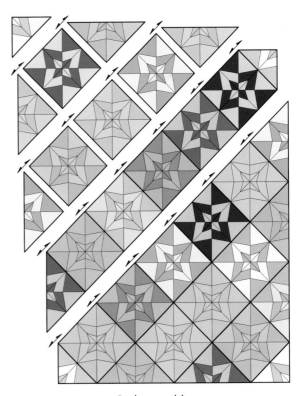

Quilt assembly

3 To create the inner border, sew the brown 3" x 42" strips together end to end to make one long strip. Measure the width of your quilt through the center and cut two strips to that length. Sew them to the top and bottom of the quilt. Press seam allowances toward the inner border.

4 Measure the length of the quilt through the center, including the borders you just added. Cut two brown strips to that length and sew to the sides of the quilt. Press.

5 Sew the green 5" x 42" strips together and repeat steps 3 and 4 to add the outer borders.

FINISHING THE QUILT

1 Piece the backing together using a horizontal seam. The backing should measure at least 60" x 73".

2 Baste, quilt as desired, and bind. For more details, see "Finishing Your Quilts" on page 81.

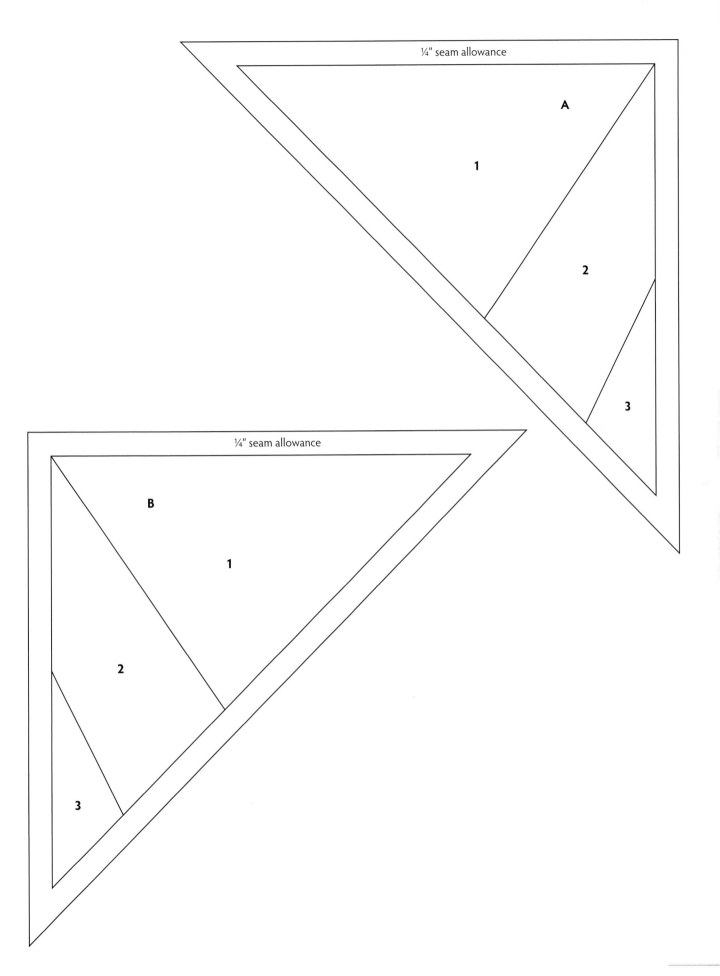

¼" seam allowance

A

1

2

3

¼" seam allowance

B

1

2

3

FINISHING YOUR QUILTS

Even though the front of your quilt will be the center of attention, the other side requires care and planning as well. The quilt backing and label offer more opportunities to let your creativity shine—even if it's not always on display.

QUILT BACKINGS

When you create the backing for your quilt, there are several different approaches you can take. Each has its own pros and cons.

Backing from Yardage

Piecing yardage is certainly the most straightforward way to create a backing. Simply purchase the amount directed by the project instructions, assemble using either a horizontal or vertical seam, and voilà—a quilt backing. This backing is quick to assemble, but since it doesn't require much creativity, it's not a huge amount of fun. If you purchase extra-wide fabric made just for backings, you won't even have to piece it.

Pieced Backing

Rather than buying the amount of backing fabric listed in the project, you can design your own pieced backing fairly simply, incorporating various fabrics or even additional patchwork for a more double-sided quilt. Many quilters consider the backing an opportunity to experiment and try new things.

To design a pieced backing, first measure the finished quilt top. Add 4" on each side to make the basting process easier and to ensure that your backing will indeed back every inch of your quilt top. Grab some graph paper to sketch it out.

First, write down the measurements for the whole backing (quilt dimensions plus 8"). Sketch out where you want to place your patchwork or secondary fabric. Determine the size of the pieced area and the size of the remaining areas. Or, you can just jump in and start piecing randomly.

Make Another Quilt Top

Another method for backing your quilts is to make a quilt top, full of more patchwork and/or blocks. Follow another pattern that will yield the same size or a slightly larger quilt top. You can use the same fabrics or even a whole new slew of fabrics that are complementary to your original quilt top.

Busy Backings

If you're just starting out or are nervous about your quilting stitches, use a busy, printed quilt backing to mask your stitches on the back of your quilt.

Get Your Scrappy On

Do you have a bunch of fabric left over from your quilt top? Start there for your backing! This is one of my favorite ways to back a quilt. It allows for so much creativity and can be a lot of fun to put together. Lay out your quilt top for size and then begin laying out your scraps to see how they will fit together. You can also use graph paper and pencil to plan out your scrappy backing if you prefer a more orderly method. The following photos show a few of my favorite ways to make simple pieced backings.

Back of "Patchwork Dreams," shown on page 20

Back of "Polaris," shown on page 44

Back of "Monterey Square," shown on page 36

QUILT LABELS

One of the most interesting things to me about quilting is the sense of history. Looking at old quilts is positively fascinating, especially when they are labeled with a year and a name that gives you a hint about their heritage. You may not intend to make a family heirloom, but your quilt just might turn into one!

You can make a quilt label in many different ways. You can embroider a label by hand or machine, and then piece it into the backing or add it with appliqué. You can use an archival pen to write a label. You can use printer-friendly fabric sheets to print a label from your computer. You can also design a label on your computer and arrange to have it printed on fabric through a custom-printing resource such as Spoonflower (see page 95).

When planning your label, always include at least two key pieces of information: your name and the year you made the quilt. From a practical point of view, this information can be very helpful if a quilt is ever lost or misplaced. And from a legacy perspective, labeling your quilt is a way to make your own contribution to quilting history.

PREPARING FOR QUILTING

Basting a quilt—securing the three layers to get them ready for quilting—is often considered a burden. For many quilters, it is their least favorite part of making a quilt. There are three ways to baste your quilt—with thread, with pins, and with basting spray. I tend to spray baste my quilts because I find it to be the most effective and speediest method, but every quilter is different, so try out the various approaches until you find your basting groove.

PREPARING TO BASTE

To prepare your quilt for thread or pin basting, follow these steps.

1 Press the finished quilt top thoroughly.

2 Iron the backing. If it's pieced, press, don't iron.

3 Remove wrinkles from the batting by tossing it in a warm dryer for 10 to 15 minutes. Trim the batting to the size of your backing.

4 Lay out your backing fabric, wrong side up, on a large table or on the floor. Tape or pin the backing so that it's smooth and somewhat taut before thread basting or pin basting. Place the batting on top, followed by your quilt top. This is your quilt sandwich, all ready for basting.

THREAD BASTING

Thread basting works best when you plan to hand quilt; if quilting by machine, basting thread can get tangled with your quilting thread.

Using white thread and an embroidery needle, take big stitches through all three layers of your quilt—and I do mean *big* stitches, at least an inch long. The bigger the stitches, the easier they'll be to pull out after you've finished quilting. Beginning in the quilt center, stitch horizontal lines throughout the quilt, and then add vertical lines. To avoid shifting of the layers, your stitches should be approximately 4" apart across the entire quilt top.

Some quilters prefer to use a contrasting thread for basting, as it's easier to find and remove after quilting, but dye from thread can transfer to fabric over time, so I recommend white thread. Once the quilting is complete, you can use a seam ripper to pull out your basting stitches.

PIN BASTING

Pins can be used by both machine and hand quilters, as they are easy to remove while quilting. Using curved safety pins or any type of rustproof safety pins, insert them one by one, making sure to penetrate all three layers of your quilt sandwich. Begin in the center of the quilt top and pin every 5" to 6". Pin basting can be time-consuming, but have patience and pin well. If you are basting on a carpeted surface, be careful not to pin your quilt to the carpet—I know, I've done that quite a few times!

SPRAY BASTING

Basting spray is a temporary adhesive that you can use much like hairspray to hold the layers of your quilt together.

1 After trimming the batting to match the backing, lay out the batting on a clean, flat surface. Smooth out any wrinkles. Place the ironed backing on top of your batting, smoothing as you go. Once your backing is all smoothed out, fold back half of the backing onto itself.

2 Spray the exposed batting with a light, even mist of basting spray, holding the can about 8" to 12" away. Slowly unfold the backing fabric over the batting, constantly smoothing any wrinkles that may begin to appear. Fold the remaining half of your backing to expose the batting and repeat the process.

Fold backing in half on top of batting.
Apply basting spray to exposed batting.

3 Flip the two layers over, leaving the batting face up. Place the quilt top on the batting and repeat the procedure with your quilt top. You're all ready to start quilting.

4 After quilting and binding are complete, wash your quilt to remove the spray adhesive. See "Caring for Your Quilt" on page 90 for washing details.

There are many ways to quilt your project. Some quilters choose to hand quilt or send their quilt off to a long-arm quilter to do the quilting for them, but I prefer to do my own machine quilting on my home sewing machine. Free-motion quilting is my favorite part of the quilting process, since it reminds me of my days as a teenage doodler.

FREE-MOTION QUILTING

Free-motion quilting is the art of guiding your quilt around under the moving needle of the sewing machine to stitch the layers of your quilt together. Mastering the technique can take a good bit of practice, but it's something that anyone with a sewing machine can do, provided the machine is in good working condition. All of the quilts in this book were free-motion quilted on my home sewing machine by yours truly.

Not sure what quilting design to use or where to stitch when you quilt? I often audition various quilting plans by printing out a couple copies of a digital photo of my quilt on printer paper. I doodle and draw designs on top of it to see what works. I typically use a roller ball pen to draw my planned stitches and go from there.

Getting started with free-motion quilting is often the hardest part, so I'm going to walk you through it step by step.

Close-up of Cathedral Windows–inspired quilting on the "Lattice of Stars" mini-quilt, shown on page 63

Meandering stipple quilting on "Refreshing Retro," shown on page 40

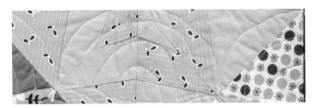

Baptist Fan quilting on "Wham," shown on page 74

Back-and-forth loose quilting from "Lattice of Stars," shown on page 60

PREPARING TO QUILT

Once your quilt is basted and ready to roll, it's time to get you and your machine ready. Here are a few important steps to follow before you get started.

1. Put a new needle in your machine. For machine quilting, I prefer using quilting or Microtex/Sharp needles, usually size 90/14, as they yield a clean, even-looking stitch.

2. Fill several bobbins before you start quilting. Depending on the size of your project, you can go through as many as 10 bobbins in one quilt.

3. Switch your sewing-machine foot to a darning foot or other free-motion foot.

4. If your machine has a needle-down button, use it! Pausing during free-motion quilting works best if you stop with the needle down.

5. Depending on how your machine acts, you may need to lower the feed dogs to allow

you to "drive" your quilt through the machine at your own pace. On my machine, I do not lower the feed dogs at all when I'm quilting. You may need to experiment with this.

6 Push your table up to a wall to keep your quilt from sliding off the back. Also, you may want to scoot your ironing board to the left of your sewing table, creating a little more surface area to support your quilt while you are working. Quilts are heavy, and if they hang off your sewing surface while quilting, it can make guiding the quilt under the needle very difficult.

7 Clear off your table, with the exception of your sewing machine. I find that as I move a quilt around while quilting, I tend to knock just about everything off my table, even my cutting mat, so I suggest clearing off your entire surface area.

To get *yourself* ready, stretch your arms and shoulders. Moving your arms in a circular motion is a great stretch that helps to engage the shoulder muscles. We have a tendency to hunch over the machine when quilting, which can cause shoulder pain. Stretching first will help prevent that.

Practice!

A great way to gain experience with free-motion quilting techniques is to make many 12" x 12" quilt sandwiches using scrap fabric. Baste and prepare them just as you would a full quilt, and practice your stitching. Muscle memory is key in free-motion quilting, so the more you practice, the better your stitches will be. You can also draw continuous-line quilting designs on paper to practice the movement of a design, or use your child's magnetic doodle pad!

LET'S QUILT!

Now that you and your machine are ready to roll, let's get started, shall we?

1 Choose a starting point. I like to start at the lower-right corner. Keep the remainder of your quilt rolled or folded for ease of movement while quilting.

Tension Headaches

In a nutshell, thread needs to flow through both the top of your machine and the bobbin at the same speed, at the very same time. Tension regulators in your machine attempt to control this flow; however, many quilters experience tension troubles when machine quilting. Batting can make the needle thread of your machine drag as it moves through the layers of your quilt, so often some adjustment is required.

Before you decide that tension is to blame for any free-motion stitch problems, first replace your needle and rethread both your top and bobbin threads. If the problem continues, refer to the manual for your sewing machine and adjust the tension as recommended.

2 Put your needle down at your starting spot and bring it up again. Pull on the top thread to bring the bobbin thread to the top. Holding the thread ends, move the needle up and down several times without moving the quilt, thus creating a knot to secure your stitches.

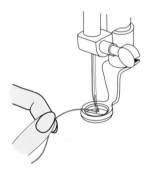

3 Begin to sew and slowly move your quilt around under the needle in the design you've chosen, keeping your foot pressed down consistently on the pedal of the machine and moving as steadily as you can. Once you've stitched a few inches away from your knot, bury your thread tails. You don't want them to get caught up in your quilting. To bury the thread tails, thread one tail with a needle and insert the threaded needle into the quilt top and into the batting—not the backing. Push the needle back

up, out of the quilt top ½" or so away from the beginning stitches. Trim the thread and repeat with the remaining thread tail.

4 Continue moving your quilt around, watching where you are going and focusing on where you will be quilting next. Rather than watching the needle, try to look ahead so you can avoid running into a previous line of quilting. As you sew, keep an eye on your thread levels, both the top thread and the bobbin thread.

5 When you run out of bobbin thread, stop. Reload your bobbin and take a close look at the quilt. Trace your quilting back about ten stitches, before your bobbin thread ran out, and gently pull out your stitches to yield top and bobbin thread tails that are approximately 1½" long. Pull both threads to the top and tie in a knot; bury the tails as in step 3.

6 To begin quilting again, place your quilt back under your machine and put the needle down where you left off, right where your knot is. Bring the needle up and pull the bobbin thread up to the quilt top. Hold your thread tails off to the side and take a few stitches in place; then quilt. Once you've quilted about 6" away, stop

with the needle down and bury the thread ends as before. You can wait and do this all at once if you prefer.

7 As you quilt, the combination of the pressure on the foot pedal and the speed of moving the quilt around will determine your stitch length. This is where practice comes in handy. As with piecing, consistency is what's important here. I find that listening to music while I'm quilting often helps me relax and move the quilt around with a consistent rhythm.

Free-motion quilting definitely takes practice, so if you feel yourself getting frustrated or are generally having a difficult time, simply turn off your machine and walk away for a bit. Take a break. Recharge. But most important, try again. *Don't give up.* You can do this! I know that we are often our own worst critics, but try to be forgiving of yourself as you learn free-motion quilting. The more you do it, the better it will get! A simple visit to the washing machine can often mask any stitches that you think are no good! Besides, we're so very close to our stitches while we're quilting that any "mistakes" seem magnified. Once you finish your quilt, it's unlikely that you'll be this close again!

Straight-Line Quilting

An alternative to free-motion quilting is straight-line quilting, using a walking foot. Many quilters really like the look of straight-line quilting and find it easier and more enjoyable than free-motion quilting. Your choice will often depend on your piecing, the fabrics used in your quilt, and the graphic look you are after.

For straight-line quilting, you'll prepare your quilt and machine in much the same way as for free-motion quilting. Instead of a darning foot, you'll use a walking foot. You may want to use a ruler and a water-soluble pen or Hera marker to mark some straight lines on your quilt to get started. You can then follow the lines of your first stitches with a seam guide to continue stitching, rather than drawing lines all over the quilt. Just be

sure to wash your quilt in cold water if you use a water-soluble marker, otherwise the lines will not wash out.

Close-up of quilting on "Diamonds Are a Girl's Best Friend" mini-quilt, shown on page 51

Close-up of quilting on "Less Is More," shown on page 32

BINDING

Binding is the last step of the quilting process, much like adding a frame to a piece of art or a photograph. There are other ways to make binding, but I will show you the method I use most often and find to be easiest: straight-grain double-fold binding. I always use 2½"-wide strips of fabric for binding, cut perpendicular to the selvage.

1 Referring to the cutting instructions for the project you're making, cut as many 2½" strips as instructed from the yardage. The strip quantity was determined by adding up the distance around the quilt, adding 12", and then dividing by 40".

2 Remove the selvage ends and sew the strips together, end to end, to create one long, continuous piece of binding. Press the seam allowances open.

3 Fold the binding in half lengthwise, wrong sides together, aligning the raw edges as you go. Press along the length of the binding. This creates a simple double-fold binding.

Fold line

4 Starting on the front of your quilt, in the middle of one of the long sides, line up the raw edges of your binding with the edges of your quilt, leaving a tail approximately 6" long. Using a ¼" seam, stitch along the edge of your quilt, stopping approximately ¼" from the first corner. Backstitch to secure your stitches, and then trim your threads.

Note: If you plan to finish your binding by machine, rather than by hand, attach the

binding to the back of your quilt instead of the front. You will fold the binding and machine stitch it on the front of the quilt. See "Finishing by Machine" on page 90 for additional details.

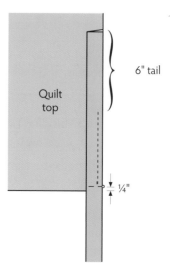

Quilt top

6" tail

¼"

5 Turn the quilt so that you will be ready to stitch down the next side. Flip your binding strip up so that it creates a 45° angle at the corner. Fold it back down on itself so that it is even with the next side, and begin stitching again.

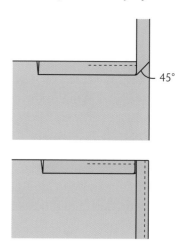

45°

6 Continue stitching around the quilt, repeating the mitering process at each corner.

7 When you get close to the tail where you started, stop stitching approximately 6" away and remove your quilt from the machine. On your ironing board, bring both binding tails together, folding them back onto themselves. With a hot iron, press to create a crease for a sewing guide.

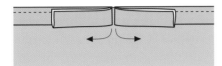

Fold each end back.
Press.

8 Unfold the binding and with right sides together, align the binding at the creases. Pin if desired, and stitch along the crease. Trim threads, and then trim excess fabric and press the seam allowances open. Refold the binding and finish sewing the binding to the quilt.

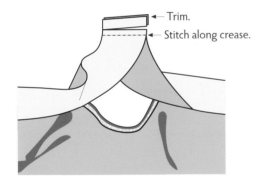

← Trim.
← Stitch along crease.

9 Use a hot iron to press the binding away from the quilt. Then flip the quilt over to press the binding onto the backing side. If you have any marks on your quilt from quilting, be sure not to touch them with the hot iron, or you could make them permanent.

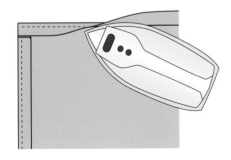

10 You can then use binding clips or straight pins to secure your binding as you finish it by hand or machine.

FINISHING BY HAND

Many quilters like to hand sew their bindings to the back of their quilts and enjoy the process as they complete the last step of quiltmaking.

1 Cut a piece of cotton thread 12" to 18" long. Make a knot at one end, and thread the unknotted end in a nice, pointy needle. I like to work with Betweens.

2 Pick a spot on your quilt to start, and anchor your knot under the fold of the binding, pulling the needle out just beyond the binding stitch line.

3 Insert your needle into the binding fold and guide the needle forward, pushing it down into your backing fabric, taking care not to go through to the quilt top. Push the needle through the backing and batting approximately 1/8" to 1/4", and then bring the needle back out again next to the fold of the binding. Pull your thread taut and continue stitching all the way around the quilt.

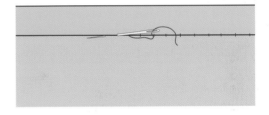

4 Miter the corners as you get to them, adding a couple stitches to anchor the mitered fold.

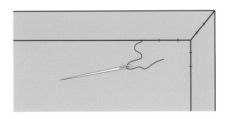

5 When you start to run out of thread, simply tie off your thread, near the raw edge of the quilt, under the binding. Bury your thread by inserting your needle under the backing and bringing it out again about ½" or so away; pull the needle out and trim the excess thread close to the backing. The thread end will be hidden under the backing.

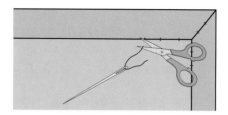

FINISHING BY MACHINE

Machine binding is a great alternative to binding by hand. I've finished many quilts this way. It's fast and easy and makes for a very secure binding on a quilt that will get a lot of use. Yes, the stitches show, but if you match the thread color to your binding or use invisible thread, your stitches will blend in nicely. You can even use a decorative stitch on your sewing machine to make the machine binding a design element of your quilt.

To machine finish binding, it's best to attach the binding to the back of the quilt so that your finishing stitches are on the quilt top.

1 Follow the steps for binding the quilt as described earlier, but sew the binding to the back of the quilt.

2 Press the binding away from the quilt and fold it over to the front to cover the stitching line. Press in place, taking care not to touch any quilting marks you may have on your quilt. Add pins or clips to hold your binding in position, or you can go without and simply use your hands to hold it in place as you go.

3 Load your bobbin with thread to match the backing fabric. Use a top thread that matches the binding fabric. You could also use invisible thread, if you prefer.

4 Stitching slowly, stitch on top of your binding, close to the fold, removing pins or clips as you get close to them. When you get to a corner, stop with the needle down, pivot the quilt, and continue. Backstitch when you reach your starting point again to secure your threads.

CARING FOR YOUR QUILT

Even though your fabrics are quilt-shop quality and manufactured by reputable companies, it's still best to treat your quilt gently when it comes to washing.

Wash your quilt to remove basting spray if you've used it and to give your quilt a vintage, puckered look. After that, wash only as needed. Hand washing your quilt is best, though it's both time-consuming and impractical for many of us. If your washing machine has a gentle cycle, that may be the best way to wash your quilt. Avoid

using strong detergents; I use baby wash because I find it to be very mild. Never dry clean a quilt!

Wet quilts need to be handled carefully. Never leave a wet quilt in the washer for too long; it can cause dyes in your fabrics to rub off on other parts of your quilt. Also, quilts can be quite heavy when wet, so try to support the weight of the quilt as best you can to avoid weakening the seams. Gently move the quilt to the dryer and run on low heat. This will prolong the life of your quilt and give you the wonderful crinkly texture of a vintage quilt.

READING QUILT PATTERNS

You can find quilt patterns almost anywhere—online, in books, and at your local quilt shop. Before you begin cutting fabric for *any* project, read all instructions thoroughly to make sure you understand the construction process. The details may vary from pattern to pattern, but terminology is similar.

TERMINOLOGY

Here's a listing of some common terms that you'll see in patterns. These explanations will help you understand what it all means.

Finished block size vs. unfinished block size. In quilting, there are two different ways to talk about block size: finished and unfinished. An unfinished block is a single block that has been assembled, but is not yet sewn into a quilt. This block will always be larger than a finished quilt block because it still has a ¼" unsewn seam allowance on all sides (½" total). The finished block size is the size of a block when sewn into a quilt top. Unfinished sizes are ½" larger than finished sizes.

Finished quilt size. Finished quilt sizes are the dimensions of the finished quilt, usually given width first and then length, before any quilting is done. It is the total of all the parts of the quilt, including any borders, assuming accurate ¼" seam allowances throughout. Sometimes the dimensions will add ½" for binding and sometimes not. In this book, I did not include the width of the binding in the finished quilt measurements.

Materials list or fabric requirements. This will describe all fabric requirements for the quilt: how many different fabrics are used and how much yardage you'll need of each one. Backing and binding yardage requirements should be listed, in addition to fabrics for the actual quilt top. If multiple size options are available with your pattern, highlight or circle the ones that apply to your choice. You don't want to accidentally misread the fabric requirements and run out of fabric! Ideally, this list will also mention any additional items you'll need, such as special rulers, templates, foundation paper, or embellishments.

Cutting instructions. This includes the number and size of pieces to cut from each fabric listed for the quilt top. The cutting dimensions always include ¼" seam allowances.

Assembly instructions. These include specific directions for sewing together the blocks and/or the quilt top.

Quilt assembly diagram or layout. This is typically a diagram showing how to arrange the quilt blocks and borders when sewing everything together to create the finished quilt top.

Finishing. Usually, the finishing details will be minimal, giving you free rein to quilt and bind your finished quilt however you would like. Occasionally, binding instructions may be included.

ABBREVIATIONS

Sometimes you'll come across "shorthand" in patterns or online. Here are some abbreviations and acronyms commonly used in the quilting world. Although they're not used in this book, you may encounter them in other patterns or in online instructions.

DSM. When you see this in patterns, it refers to a domestic (home) sewing machine.

FE or F8. This stands for a fat eighth of fabric, which is based on ⅛-yard cuts. A typical ⅛ yard measures 4½" x 42". A fat eighth is 9" x 21", twice as long, but half as wide.

FG. This is short for flying-geese unit, which is a rectangle made up of one quarter-square triangle and two half-square triangles. (See "Lattice of Stars" on page 61 for a block that includes flying-geese units.)

FMQ. This is my favorite—free-motion machine quilting. I love FMQ! (See page 85 for details.)

FQ. This indicates a fat quarter, which is an 18" x 21" cut of fabric. It is twice the length of a typical quarter yard, which measures 9" x 42", but it's only half as wide.

HST. This is shorthand for half-square-triangle units. These are squares pieced from two triangles. The two triangles are usually from squares that have been cut in half diagonally from corner to corner.

QAYG. Quilt-as-you-go is a method of quilting in which you layer and quilt individual blocks with batting before they are assembled into a quilt top.

QST. These are quarter-square-triangle units, which are squares pieced from four triangles. The triangles are usually from squares that have been cut into quarters diagonally from corner to corner (cut diagonally in both directions).

WOF. This abbreviation stands for "width of fabric," and represents the width of the fabric from selvage to selvage. If the cutting instructions say to cut a strip "2" x wof," this means to cut a 2"-wide strip perpendicular to the selvages. The selvages are then usually trimmed off. Some patterns simply list the width of fabric as 42" even though it may be slightly more or less than that. For the projects in this book, yardage calculations are based on 42"-wide fabric with a usable length of 40" per strip after prewashing and removing selvages.

RESOURCES FOR MODERN QUILTERS

One of the most amazing things about modern quilting is the community of quilters you can find and connect with, both in person and on the Internet.

All across the United States and in many other parts of the world, you can locate chapters of the Modern Quilt Guild (MQG). The MQG is a great resource for finding other like-minded quilters, sharing your projects with others who "get it," and learning and honing your craft. You can find a complete list of the MQG chapters at www.themodernquiltguild.com. Your local quilt shop may have information on other quilt guilds in your area, as well.

The Internet is a fabulous place to find other modern quilters. Many quilters keep blogs as online diaries of their work as well as for networking with other quilters. The two primary blog platforms are Blogger (www.blogger.com) and Wordpress (www.wordpress.org). I use Blogger and have found it extremely user friendly. If you are considering starting a quilting blog and need a little help, your local library should have plenty of guidebooks about both platforms. One book I highly recommend is *Blogging for Bliss* (Lark Crafts, 2009) by Tara Frey; it's a great guide to building a craft blog. I love having a blog; it's an online scrapbook of sorts, containing the stories behind my quilts as well as my creative journey as a quilter.

A Word about Instagram

Another great place to share your quilts with others is Instagram. Instagram is a phone app that's become an addiction for many quilters, allowing them to share works in progress as well as fabric splurges and finished quilts. You can also use descriptive hashtags to connect with other like-minded quilters, like #paperpiecing or #freemotionquilting.

If you're not the type who enjoys writing about your work, you can always utilize Flickr, an online photo-sharing site partnered with Snapfish for ease of printing. On Flickr, you can post your photos in various groups—some focused on a particular fabric designer or manufacturer, others geared toward a particular kind of quilt or style, like the Fresh Modern Quilts group or the Modern Mini-Quilts group. Each group has its own forum and message board to facilitate chatting with other members of the group.

Flickr is also the home base for many modern swaps and virtual bees. One of the first things you'll notice about modern quilters online is that we like to make things for each other! It's a very collaborative community, and swaps and virtual bees are a great example of that spirit.

SWAPS

In a Flickr swap, you'll find an entire group dedicated to the swap. Most swaps have a particular focus, like the swap "Pillow Talk," which focused on making and swapping quilted pillow covers. Another swap I've participated in, "Spicing Up the Kitchen," focused on sewn items for your kitchen, such as pot holders, table runners, and the like. People who are interested in joining the swap sign up via a discussion thread in the group's message board, and the swap leaders, often called the "swap mamas," match up secret partners for the swap. You will usually fill out a questionnaire of some kind to assist your secret partner in understanding your likes and dislikes, and you can also view your partner's Favorites in Flickr for further inspiration and insight.

Before You Join

Before you join a bee or a swap, it's best to get in some practice. Make some full-sized quilts. Make some mini-quilts and pillows. Take photos as you go and begin to build your Flickr photostream and profile. Join some groups on Flickr and mark your favorite photos as you come across them. Participate in discussions. Build on your experience before you join a swap or virtual bee, and then you'll truly get the most out of sharing that experience with others.

QUILTING BEES

Many years ago, our grandmothers and their grandmothers who lived in close proximity to each other often gathered to work on group quilts in a setting called a quilting bee. Women would often spend the afternoon working together to complete a quilt in a faster time frame than a single person could. Traditional quilting bees still exist today, often taking place for fundraising efforts. While speed was certainly a benefit of working in a bee setting, the social benefits of participating in a group also played a large part in their popularity.

With the advent of the Internet and its prevalence within the modern quilting community, virtual quilting bees have become easy to form and extremely popular. Flickr is full of bees, and there's a group called Quilting Bee Blocks where you will find many discussions on how to join a quilting bee. Several virtual quilting bees are seasonal or quarterly, allowing you to "join" or participate as you have time—a great advantage for career women or busy moms. One great quarterly bee is the 4 x 5 Modern Quilt Bee. You are in a small group and sew a block for each member of your group during a four- to six-week period.

How does a virtual quilting bee work? One member organizes the bee, which can include anywhere from 10 to 16 participants. Bee members make blocks and send them to the others as needed, since most members don't live in close proximity to each other. Each member selects a month of the year in which she or he chooses what kind of block the members will make, what the finished size should be, and so forth. This member becomes the "queen bee" for the month. The queen bee may send specific fabric for each bee member to work with, although there are plenty of bees that involve working from each individual's own personal stash of fabric.

Once bee members finish their blocks for the month, they send them to the queen bee. It's then up to the queen bee to assemble and finish the quilt. Sometimes, when making a large quilt, a bee member may repeat the same block when his or her turn comes around again. The finished quilt belongs to the queen bee, who can use it as a gift, a family heirloom—you name it!

Golden Rules of Swapping and Bees

- Make something you're proud of.
- Send on time!
- Be mindful of your partner's taste; if the person isn't into batiks, don't use them! Save them for another project.
- Beef up your Flickr profile before joining any swaps or bees—be sure to add pictures to your Favorites and post a wide variety of photos of your own work.

FABRIC MANUFACTURERS

Andover Fabrics
www.andoverfabrics.com

Art Gallery Fabrics
www.artgalleryfabrics.com

Dear Stella Fabrics
www.dearstelladesign.com

Free Spirit Fabrics/Westminster Fibers
www.freespiritfabric.com

Michael Miller Fabrics
www.michaelmillerfabrics.com

Moda Fabrics
www.unitednotions.com

Robert Kaufman Fabrics
www.robertkaufman.com

Timeless Treasures Fabrics
www.ttfabrics.com

Windham Fabrics
www.windhamfabrics.com

ONLINE FABRIC SHOPS

Fabric.com
www.fabric.com

Fabric Shack
www.fabricshack.com

Fabricworm
www.fabricworm.com

Fat Quarter Shop
www.fatquartershop.com

Hawthorne Threads
www.hawthornethreads.com

Pink Castle Fabrics
www.pinkcastlefabrics.com

Pink Chalk Fabrics
www.pinkchalkfabrics.com

Sew, Mama, Sew
www.sewmamasew.com

SOURCES FOR NOTIONS AND OTHER ITEMS

Jo-Ann Fabric and Crafts
www.joann.com

Sew for Less
www.sewforless.com

Simplicity
www.simplicity.com

Spoonflower
www.spoonflower.com

Elizabeth Dackson is a quilter and self-proclaimed fabric addict. She designs quilt patterns found both on her blog, Don't Call Me Betsy (www.dontcallmebetsy.com), and in various quilting publications, including *Quiltmaker*, *Modern Quilts Unlimited*, *International Quilt Festival: Quilt Scene*, *Quilty*, *Love of Quilting*, and *Fat Quarterly*. She is also an active member of the Tampa Modern Quilt Guild. Elizabeth lives in Florida with her husband, son, and neurotic beagle.

ACKNOWLEDGMENTS

Thank you so much to my wonderful husband, John Dackson, for all of your support throughout this journey. You've been so amazing and I cannot thank you enough. I am a lucky lady to be able to call you mine. Thank you to my sweet little boy, Ryan, for cheering me on and for all of your help with fabric and color selection. I love you!

Thank you also to everyone at Martingale for believing in me and this book.

Thank you to Andover Fabrics, Art Gallery Fabrics, Dear Stella Fabrics, Free Spirit Fabrics, Michael Miller Fabrics, Moda Fabrics, Robert Kaufman Fabrics, Timeless Treasures Fabrics, and Windham Fabrics for providing beautiful fabrics for me to work with, and to Pellon for supplying wonderful batting for my quilts, as well as Aurifil for the amazing threads.

Finally, thank you to my dear quilty friends and all of my blog readers. Thank you for all of the support you've given me and all the inspiration you continually share. I appreciate each and every one of you!